The Panthers Can't
Save Us Now

The Jacobin series features short interrogations of politics, economics, and culture from a socialist perspective, as an avenue to radical political practice. The books offer critical analysis and engagement with the history and ideas of the Left in an accessible format.

The series is a collaboration between Verso Books and Jacobin magazine, which is published quarterly in print and online at jacobinmag.com.

The Panthers Can't Save Us Now

*Debating Left Politics
and Black Lives Matter*

by
CEDRIC JOHNSON

VERSO
London • New York

First published by Verso 2022
Collection © Verso 2022
Contributions © Contributors 2022

1 3 5 7 9 10 8 6 4 2

Verso
UK: 6 Meard Street, London W1F 0EG
US: 20 Jay Street, Suite 1010, Brooklyn, NY 11201
versobooks.com

Verso is the imprint of New Left Books

ISBN-13: 978-1-83976-630-5
ISBN-13: 978-1-83976-631-2 (UK EBK)
ISBN-13: 978-1-83976-632-9 (US EBK)

British Library Cataloguing in Publication Data
A catalogue record for this book is available from the British Library

Library of Congress Control Number: 2021948553

Typeset in Fournier MT by Hewer Text UK Ltd, Edinburgh
Printed and bound by CPI Group (UK) Ltd, Croydon CR0 4YY

Contents

Preface:
The Triumph of Black Lives Matter and Neoliberal Redemption

Cedric Johnson

Draped in Ghanaian kente cloth, a fabric popularized by Afrocentric nationalists during the late 1980s, a dozen or so congressional Democrats knelt in a moment of silence before unveiling their Justice in Policing legislation. It was June 8, 2020, exactly two weeks after George Floyd was killed by Minneapolis police, and in the midst of an unprecedented wave of protests that had already swept more than 500 US towns and cities in all fifty states, along with scores of demonstrations of solidarity globally. Led by Karen Bass, Congressional Black Caucus chair, and House Speaker Nancy Pelosi, the congress members embraced the language and tone of Black Lives Matter protests, with some lecturing on the "original sin" of slavery, and South Carolina congressman James Clyburn adding that Floyd's death was "just a continuation" of a long and unbroken history of American racism. Even senators Kamala Harris and Cory Booker, former presidential hopefuls, traded in their previous roles as tough-on-crime enforcers and adopted the histrionic rhetoric of popular anti-racism. This was perhaps the perfect valence to mount the center-right Democratic renewal, especially after a botched campaign to impeach Donald Trump, and the social democratic left challenge of Bernie Sanders's second bid for the party's nomination. That moment was a triumph for Black Lives Matter activists, but it was already clear that once the plumes of tear gas dissipated and compassion fatigue set in, the real beneficiaries would be the neoliberal Democrats and the capitalist blocs they serve. Indeed, nearly all of the Democratic leadership who "took a knee" against racist policing have openly opposed Medicare for All, free higher education, and the expansion of other public goods. Their technical reforms to reduce excessive force incidents and prosecute police for misconduct are the perfect way of displaying commitment to racial justice, while perpetuating the very pro-market logics and class relations that "broken windows" policing and mass incarceration were invented to protect.

Adolph Reed Jr.'s "How Racial Disparity Does Not Help Make Sense of Patterns of Police Violence"[1] should be read again and often during this moment of resurgent Black Lives Matter sentiment, precisely because he so clearly names the limitations of anti-racism as a way of thinking about the problems of carceral power, and cautions against any left-progressive politics that separates racism from historical processes and political economy. As Reed notes, "antiracism is not a different sort of egalitarian alternative to a class politics but *is* a class politics itself." Furthermore, anti-racist politics is essentially "the left wing of neoliberalism in that its sole metric of social justice is opposition to disparity in the distribution of goods and bads in the society, an ideal that naturalizes the outcomes of capitalist market forces so long as they are equitable along racial (and other identitarian) lines." Of course, I can already hear some friends of mine, academic colleagues and activists alike, who will grumble and cry foul, quickly asserting the presence of this or that tendency that embodies the true radical spirit of Black Lives Matter. Others will likely point to the scale of recent protests as evidence of a new moment, a turning point that will yield massive substantive reforms. Like the Occupy Wall Street protests before, however, Black Lives Matter is more of a sentiment than a fully formed political force. Let's not forget that it was born as a hashtag, and while it has provided a powerful banner for longer-standing organizations and legislative campaigns working to reverse the social toll of carceral expansion, the liberal character of the hashtag should be more apparent now than ever.

During summer 2020, we all witnessed the readiness with which different class layers embraced the slogan. Some activists seized upon the images of mass protests as evidence of a gathering political will, but the amorphous nature of Black Lives Matter, which Reed rightly compared to the Black Power slogan from decades earlier, and the facile expressions of unity in endless memes and viral videos of police-civilian line dances conceal substantive political differences among protestors and within broader US publics. While a slim majority of Americans now believe police are more likely to use excessive force against blacks than other groups, millions more do not share the most militant calls to defund or dismantle police departments voiced by some activists.[2] Most Americans are upset by police killings, but they also want more effective policing. In recent years, satisfaction with policing has strengthened among all ethnic and racial groups, including African Americans (from 50 percent "at least somewhat satisfied" in 2015 to 72 percent in 2020).

Black Lives Matter sentiment is essentially a militant expression of racial liberalism. Such expressions are not a threat but rather a bulwark to the neoliberal project that has obliterated the social wage, gutted public sector employment and worker pensions, undermined collective bargaining and union power, and rolled out an expansive carceral apparatus—all developments that have adversely affected black workers and communities. Sure, some activists are calling for defunding police departments and decarceration, but as a popular slogan, "Black Lives Matter" is a cry for full recognition within the established terms of liberal democratic capitalism. And the ruling class agrees.

During the so-called Blackout Tuesday social media event, corporate giants like Walmart and Amazon widely condemned the killing of George Floyd and other policing excesses. Gestural anti-racism was already evident at Amazon, which in February 2020 flew the red, black and green black liberation flag over its Seattle headquarters. The world's wealthiest man, Jeff Bezos, even took the time to respond personally to customer upset that Amazon expressed sympathy with the George Floyd protestors. " 'Black Lives Matter' doesn't mean other lives don't matter," the Amazon CEO wrote. "I have a 20-year-old son, and I simply don't worry that he might be choked to death while being detained one day. It's not something I worry about. Black parents can't say the same." Bezos also pledged $10 million in support of "social justice organizations," namely the American Civil Liberties Union Foundation, the Brennan Center for Justice, the Equal Justice Initiative, the Lawyers' Committee for Civil Rights under Law, the National Association for the Advancement of Colored People (NAACP), the National Bar Association, the National Museum of African American History and Culture, the National Urban League, the Thurgood Marshall College Fund, the United Negro College Fund, and Year Up. The leadership of Warner, Sony Music and Walmart each committed $100 million to similar organizations. The protests provided a public relations windfall for Bezos and his ilk. Only weeks before Floyd's killing, Amazon, Instacart, Grubhub and other delivery-based firms, which became crucial for commodity circulation during the national shelter-in-place, faced mounting pressure from labor activists over their inadequate protections, low wages, lack of health benefits and other poor working conditions. Corporate anti-racism is the perfect egress from these labor conflicts. Black Lives Matter to the front office, as long as they don't demand a living wage, personal protective equipment and quality health care.

Perhaps the most important point in Reed's 2016 essay is his insistence that Black Lives Matter and cognate notions like the New Jim Crow are empirically and analytically wrong and advance an equally wrongheaded set of solutions. He does not deny the fact of racial disparity in criminal justice but points us toward a deeper causation and the need for more fulsome political interventions. Racism alone cannot fully explain the expansive carceral power in our midst, which, as Reed notes, is "the product of an approach to policing that emerges from an imperative to contain and suppress the pockets of economically marginal and sub-employed working-class populations produced by revanchist capitalism." Most Americans have now rejected the worst instances of police abuse, but not the institution of policing, nor the consumer society it services. As we should know too well by now, white guilt and black outrage have limited political currency, and neither has ever been a sustainable basis for building the kind of popular and legislative majorities needed to actually contest entrenched power in any meaningful way.

The wave of mass protests that George Floyd's death provoked is not reducible to Black Lives Matter, but was also a consequence of the broader COVID-19 pandemic and real hardship of the shelter-in-place order, which was necessary for public health, but, without adequate sustained federal relief, produced mass layoffs, food pantries hard pressed to keep up with unprecedented need, and broad anxiety among many Americans about their bleak near-term employment prospects. The looting that broke out in many cities the weekend after Floyd's murder was not like the ghetto rebellions of the sixties, Los Angeles in 1992, or even Ferguson and Baltimore in recent years. The looters were multiracial and intergenerational, and they targeted downtowns and central shopping districts like Santa Monica's Third Street Promenade, Manhattan's Times Square and Chicago's State

Street and the Magnificent Mile. Throughout the 2020 protests, mainstream civil rights leaders, some Black Lives Matter activists, the corporate punditry and many other Americans frequently and loudly drew a distinction between the righteousness of peaceful protestors and the "violence" and lawlessness of looters and rioters. That posture, like hyperbolic claims about the primacy of the color line, will continue to defer the kind of public goods that might actually help the most dispossessed of all races and ethnicities, who are the most likely to be routinely surveilled, harassed, arrested, convicted, incarcerated and condemned as failures—the collateral damage of the American dream.

Acknowledgments

Writing can often be a rather solitary enterprise, but thinking is always collaborative. So many people contributed to shaping the essays collected here. The lead essay, "The Panthers Can't Save Us Now," began as an impromptu lecture at the 2015 Historical Materialism Conference in New York. I was slated to do the closing plenary session, but when my co-presenters canceled, Paul Heideman asked if I'd be willing to close out the conference solo. The conference convened less than a week after the death of Freddie Gray following his arrest by Baltimore police. My lecture laid out provisional arguments about the perils of Black Power nostalgia, the class character of the carceral regime, the promise and limitations of popular struggles against policing, and how this might all be connected to left anti-capitalist politics.

Vivek Chibber invited me to expand that lecture into an essay for the inaugural issue of the journal *Catalyst*, which he co-founded with Robert Brenner. I owe a huge debt of gratitude to Bob and Vivek for all the editorial support, advice, criticism, and encouragement they offered as I developed the essay. Sincerest thanks to Bhaskar Sunkara as well. In his role as editor and publisher of *Jacobin* and *Catalyst*, he has been a consistent supporter of my work over the last half decade.

Suzi Weissman, Barbara Garson, Robert Capistrano, and the members of the Daniel Singer Millennium Prize Foundation made my year when they recognized my essay with the 2017 award. Spending time with them at the Left Forum was truly one of the highlights of the last decade for me. I also wish to thank the editors of *New Politics*, namely Nancy Holmstrom and Saulo Manuel Colón Zavala, who proposed doing a symposium on the "Panthers" essay. Thanks as well to Mia Charlene White, Kim Moody, Touré F. Reed, and Jay Arena for taking the time to critically engage my work.

I want to express my deepest, heartfelt thanks to Carlos García, Saioa Sáez, Jorge Rodríguez, and Itxaso Txuntxurreta, the editorial collective of Libros Corrientes in Madrid. In 2020, they published a Spanish-language collection based on the essay "The Panthers Can't Save Us Now" and critical responses to that piece. I am forever grateful for their generosity, editorial labors, and comradeship.

Sincerest thanks to Asher Spencer-Dupuy, Jeanne Tao, and Duncan Ranslem for their respective editorial labors on this project. Many friends, comrades, and fellow travelers shaped my contributions to this volume. Sincerest thanks to Zhandarka Kurti, Stephen Ward, Thomas J. Adams, Donnell Walton, Megan French-Marcelin, Adolph Reed Jr., Adrienne Dixson, Justin Rose, O. Nicholas Robertson, Connor Kilpatrick, Matthew Birkhold, Shanti Singham, Johari Jabir,

Andy Clarno, Kenneth Warren, Preston Smith, Nicholas Brown, Dean Robinson, Nikol Alexander-Floyd, Walter Benn Michaels, Dustin Guastella, and Todd Cronan. Thank you for commenting on my earliest ramblings. You all provided encouragement when I needed it most and pushed me past my own limitations and toward the best articulations and insights. I am forever indebted to you.

Last but not least, I wish to thank my family for being a constant source of support and inspiration. My partner, Sekile, has weathered many personal and professional storms with me over the years, sharing sacrifices and victories. My children—Cabral, Zora, and Kimathi—are a constant reminder of what is most important in life and give me hope that a better, more just world is possible.

Introduction

Vivek Chibber

This collection is released at an interesting moment in American politics. It is organized around a provocative essay by Cedric Johnson, originally published in early 2017. The essay was immediately recognized as an important intervention, winning the coveted Daniel Singer Prize that year and triggering an intense and wide-ranging debate, much of which is brought together in this book. There was a sense of urgency to the debate because it came in the midst of a growing anti-racist movement in the United States, centered around, but not confined to, the issue of police brutality and mass incarceration. The questions that the left had to face were how this movement would be organized, and what its strategic perspective might be. Johnson wrote his intervention in response to what he recognized as a dominant trend in intellectual circles to seek inspiration and guidance from the anti-racist movement of the 1960s. If the goal was to seek inspiration from Black Power, the Black Panthers were the natural choice. No organization in that corner of anti-racist mobilization grew as fast or was as effective as they; and none has come close to occupying such a conspicuous place in the popular imagination.

Johnson's project was, in part, to interrogate the viability of the Panthers as an organizational model and a strategic actor. But more directly, it was to question the political vision of Black Power writ large, and by extension, to critique the present-day tendency to resurrect it as a model. Finally, Johnson sought to place both moments in their historical context—to examine the social roots of Black Power, to ask why particular strata find it particularly appealing, and then to propose a strategy that would find greater scope and political success. This was the goal of the essay, and the responses to it tend to orbit around those very issues.

Since Johnson published the original essay, the urgency of the issues it addresses has only intensified. The Black Lives Matter movement, launched in 2013 in response to the deaths of several young black men at the hands of the police, gained steam in 2014 after New York City police murdered Eric Garner in July of that year. While those deaths triggered a massive public outcry and a significant anti-racist mobilization across the United States, the response was dwarfed by what was to come several years later. On May 25, 2020, Derek Chauvin, a Minneapolis police officer, killed George Floyd, a working-class African American, in plain view of several bystanders. Those present filmed the entire gruesome incident, stretching over several minutes, in which Chauvin, using his knee, strangled Floyd to death. His murder triggered a national outcry even greater than the one that had followed Garner's death. Urban centers across the United

States erupted in protest, from the largest coastal megalopolises to small Midwestern towns; it was a movement that spanned all demographic groups and classes. Within days the officers involved in the incident were placed under arrest. In April 2021 Chauvin was found guilty on three counts of murder and manslaughter in a Minnesota court; he was ultimately sentenced to twenty-two and a half years in prison.

The guilty verdict was an important step forward in the struggle against racism and particularly against police brutality. Of course, the fact that Chauvin's murder of Floyd was recorded and made public had a lot to do with the outcome. It just happened that this particular incident unfolded in full view, giving bystanders the chance to film it, while so many others go unnoticed and unaddressed. Many commentators have offered that it was the video that ensured that this time the police would not get away unscathed. But such a conclusion is overdrawn. One only has to think back to 1991, when video surfaced of several officers brutally beating a black man named Rodney King. This was one of the earliest instances where video of police brutality against a black man was made publicly available. While there was no internet on which to view it at will, the video was played on a near-constant loop on every television network. Like the murder of George Floyd, the incident triggered a national outcry and a wave of urban riots. And then, too, the officers involved were arrested and tried for the crime. But in that case, they were found innocent, despite the obvious criminality of the act, the dubious character of the officers involved, and, above all, the visceral immediacy of the recording itself. That video could not bring justice for King in the way the later one seemed to for Floyd.

The difference in legal outcomes and the scale of the ensuing mobilizations speaks to the contrast in social contexts. Rodney King's mauling by the police came in the depths of the neoliberal era, when social movements were in a deep freeze and the political culture generally was moving rapidly to the right. The national uprising in the wake of the April 1992 court verdict was considerable, but it was swimming against a much more powerful political current. And there is the fact that it was barely a generation after the passage of the 1965 Voting Rights Act, the high point of the civil rights movement—enough time for the evils of racism to be widely acknowledged, but not enough for such sentiments to percolate deeper into the culture.

In the thirty years since the King verdict, much has changed. Floyd's murder came at a time when movements were emerging from a long slumber; unlike the time of King's assault, neoliberalism is in retreat against a rising populist sentiment; and even while racial oppression still has a powerful anchor in the political economy, the cultural acknowledgment of its evils is far wider—much deeper than it was a generation ago. This is no doubt the reason the political mobilization in the wake of Floyd's death was so extensive. It grew on more fertile soil, had more media coverage, and drew on a deeper reservoir of popular support. Even while it jogged memories of the 1992 riots, this uprising was orders of magnitude greater in scope and size. It is widely regarded as the biggest social mobilization since the civil rights movement, which might very well be true—the mobilization against the Vietnam War being the only comparable case.

Given the obvious parallels of the current movement with those of the 1960s, it is not surprising that its participants draw on the memories and language of that era. Indeed, some have gone even further into the past, describing the struggles today as a "Third Reconstruction"—invoking the tumultuous years after the Civil War. And in both of these gestures, the basic intuition has much to recommend it. The mobilization today is, as it was then, over basic freedoms for African Americans; there is a demand, as there was then, for the recognition of fundamental rights and freedoms; and there is also a grim understanding that it will require a direct confrontation with the power centers defending the status quo. With regard to the more proximate reference point—the civil rights movement—there is also the important fact that the generation that participated in it is still alive and active, invoking its legacy and urging that the current struggles are but its extension. The fact that many African Americans are now prominently placed in media, the academic world, and politics gives them ample means to frame the discussion in just this fashion.

But while there are grounds to seek parallels between the earlier movements and this one, there are also powerful reasons to question such a framing. The most important of these is that in the interim, the African American population has itself undergone profound changes—perhaps more significant than the changes in the years between Reconstruction and the 1960s. Specifically, the intervening half century has witnessed a significant transformation of the class structure of black Americans, in which there is now a substantial middle class, a significant layer of establishment politicians, and an influential stratum of mainstream intellectuals. And more recently there has also been some increase of African American representation in corporate boardrooms, rounding out the process of class formation. This does not alter the fact that the majority is still not only housed within the working class but also at its poorer end; that the latter sections are thrown in greater numbers into the penal system; or that they tend to suffer more from the various physical and social consequences of poverty than working-class whites. But it does mean that there is a substantial section of the African American population that has entered the higher echelons of the income scales as well as the central political and cultural institutions.

Much of the debate on race, especially within the left, revolves around the significance of this development. The conventional wisdom in the mainstream, and also on the left, minimizes its importance. On this view, there is a "black community," all of which suffers the indignities and liabilities of racial subordination; this occurs to varying degrees, no doubt, but the commonalities across income groups are taken to swamp any differences among them. Indeed, to deny this common condition of racial subordination is itself viewed as a symptom of the racial bias among intellectuals and policy makers—or in the case of black intellectuals, a blind spot to the conditions of their compatriots. In the modal expression of this view, a black American is as vulnerable to suffering from racial domination as any other, regardless of his or her income or wealth. This is claimed to be borne out if you examine the data on just about any social indicator, whether it is income, poverty, incarceration, asset ownership, housing—on every dimension, blacks do worse than whites at corresponding income levels. This being the case, whatever differentiation has occurred within black America, it is of less significance than the group-level liabilities its members face by virtue of their common racial status. Hence, the argument goes, the basic division in society is between races, not classes.

Cedric Johnson is among a small handful of intellectuals in the United States, and an even smaller number of black intellectuals, who are critical of this framework. On his view, racial politics is firmly imbricated in the underlying dynamics of the capitalist political economy. It does not have a life, or a logic, of its own. Its anchor in the political economy is expressed in many ways, but two stand out in Johnson's analysis. The first is that the contours of economic and political opportunity for black Americans have been centrally governed by the evolution of the economy, the dynamics of which are themselves independent of the racial hierarchy. Thus, the enormous gains made in the 1960s and '70s were themselves fueled by the epochal economic expansion in the industrial heartland, which generated employment opportunities that the American working class had never seen. Working-class blacks, many of whom had migrated to the North as the Southern plantation economy mechanized in the 1940s, certainly had to fight for their access to these opportunities, but the latter were a precondition to any economic advancement, thus constituting an enabling condition for whatever gains they were able to secure. Without economic expansion, the class consequences of the civil rights movement would have been very different. Conversely, Johnson argues, the precipitous decline in black economic fortunes was forced by the dramatic slowdown of economic growth in the 1970s, the consequent weakening of the labor movement, and the strangulation of fiscal revenues in urban America. Racial attitudes made matters worse, but they could only work within the limits set by the economic forces. Any attempt to understand the fortunes of black America independently of the political economy is, in Johnson's view, doomed from the start.

The second way in which racial politics is linked to the capitalist economy is in its political consequences. The internal differentiation of the black class structure has had a direct bearing on the articulation of the political demands. In the early postwar years, one of the most important consequences of the Great Migration was an enormous expansion of the black working class—in the Northern cities, of course, but also in the South. Because this entry into the ranks of waged labor occurred during a period of rapid growth and the expansion of the trade union movement, demands for racial justice from the 1930s to the 1960s had a conspicuous working-class inflection. As the recent historiography of the civil rights movement has shown, its strategic perspective gave central importance to economic rights, viewing them as the precondition to the fulfillment of formal political rights.[1] Even if one follows veteran organizer Bayard Rustin in noting a break in the movement's perspective and social base after 1965, the fact remains that the movement for racial justice had a firm social democratic impulse into the 1970s.[2]

This impulse weakened pari passu with the decline of labor. Whereas the progressive movement at midcentury took economic redistribution as the essential precondition for political equality, the discourse around race began to shift slowly but steadily during the final two decades. Johnson himself has written a superb analysis of the debates within the black political leadership in the early 1970s, when the class basis of black politics had already begun to shift, becoming increasingly top-heavy and elite driven.[3] Still, this was not the dominant trend in the '70s, and most black political leaders hewed to a largely redistributive agenda. But a decade later, the drift away from the progressive core was more evident. Political demands gradually shifted away from their marriage to universalistic and redistributive ones, and toward a narrower discourse that focused on representation and political inclusion. This change was, in Johnson's view, a direct consequence of the waning influence of the black working class on those who claimed to speak for them. The pressure that had once come from below was now displaced by the aspirations of an emerging class of brokers and politicos who adopted the rhetoric of empowerment and justice for their own ends.

It was natural that in this process, the language of Black Power became increasingly detached from mass politics. Both dimensions of class influence on black political life strengthened over time. A rather small black middle class had, by the 2010s, become quite substantial by historical standards, and the stratum of brokers and political operatives ballooned to orders of magnitude beyond what it was in 1965. This emerging class took hold of the rhetoric of the civil rights era and harnessed it to its own class aspirations, which were entirely distinct from the masses of black Americans. By the time the Black Lives Matter movement erupted in 2013–14, the language of Black Power had become more a symbolic gesture among NGOs and the academic conference circuit, and less a strategic perspective for organized struggle. In other words, it had been domesticated by the class of black professionals and politicos incubated by neoliberalism.

For anyone even remotely familiar with the history of twentieth-century nationalism, this story should be all too familiar. Elites speaking in the name of an oppressed group mobilize the language of community and common condition, in order to put it at the service of their own narrow interests. This was the story of so many anti-colonial movements, and also that of ethnic and racial movements within nation-states. Race politics in the United States is no exception, and indeed fits seamlessly into that broader pattern. But it is testimony to the parlous state of political debate in the United States, especially in the analysis of race, that Johnson's view is not only a minority current, but is considered controversial—even, or I should say, *particularly*, on the left. But then, this is not surprising if we examine the social composition of left currents, which are largely the same as those articulating the rhetoric of Black Power today—academics, nonprofits, political operators and a thin layer of professionals, largely unmoored from the working class. Within this grouping, a narrow and quite conservative identity politics reigns supreme, even while its political discourse revolves around demands for emancipation, empowerment, social justice and the like.

Hence, Johnson's call for class solidarity among working people of all races and ethnicity is, quite astonishingly, met with skepticism; his insistence that it is working-class blacks who bear the brunt of racial oppression, and not black Americans as a whole, elicits outrage; and his insistence that white workers endure a life of oppression, and not the purported benefits of "privilege," is met with outright disdain. Some of these reactions are represented in this book, but many others can be found in the larger debate around his essay. They reflect a political culture in which debates around policy and strategy are almost entirely hegemonized by professional strata, extending across the racial divide.

It was once taken for granted on the left that if the struggle against racism was to be one against racial *oppression*, it would have to center on economic demands—jobs, housing, health care, pensions, and so on. And in order to attain these ends, that it would have to be, in the first instance a movement led by poor and working people, since elite groupings within minority populations had little or no interest in advancing these issues. Secondly, if they were to be successful, they would have to be interracial, not sectional. This should be obvious, but it needs to be spelled out—a nationalist mobilization by small minorities, whether brown or black, will never gather the leverage to make a real dent on economic demands against the most powerful capitalist class in the world. It will have to be a movement that elicits the support from, and participation by, the working class as a whole. Hence Johnson's bracing conclusion: that the invocation of Black Power, and the nationalist sentiment that it expresses, cannot substitute for a real political analysis. So long as it refuses to acknowledge the real constraints on the vast majority of black Americans, it will serve primarily as theater, not strategy.

Johnson's argument is not only a sober analysis of the moment, but a call for the left to embrace the values and the strategic perspective that once enabled it to become a mighty political force. It is still very much a minority view within the emerging left—but one that is gaining in traction as progressives gain in strength. Whether it becomes the common sense of progressives, as it once was, is still very much up in the air. This collection plays an important role in pushing us toward that elusive goal.

1

The Panthers Can't Save Us Now

Anti-policing Struggles and the Limits of Black Power

Cedric Johnson

In early December 2013, Senegalese artist Issa Samb donned a black leather jacket and beret, grasped a spear in his left hand and an M1 carbine rifle in his right, and settled into a rattan throne. Samb's live performance replicated the 1967 photo of Huey Newton, carefully staged by Eldridge Cleaver in the *Ramparts* magazine office, that would become the most iconic representation of Black Panther Party militancy and internationalism. Samb chose to recreate the famous image in an abandoned storefront that had previously housed a Harold's Chicken restaurant, along Chicago's Garfield Boulevard. His performance was part of a weeklong series of events hosted by the University of Chicago to commemorate the 1969 police killings of Illinois Panthers Mark Clark and Fred Hampton and to encourage reflection on the party's legacy. Titled "The Best Marxist Is Dead," Samb's performance might be read as a commentary on the perils of Black

Power nostalgia and as a call for the renewed critique of capitalism within black public life and a radical left politics keenly attuned to new historical conditions.

Samb's performance is an homage that evokes Newton's notion of revolutionary suicide—that the true show of radical commitment is the willingness to dedicate one's full energy and time, and potentially one's life, to revolutionary struggle. The performance title and Newton's radical pledge are both in keeping with the Panther quip "The only good pig is a dead one." If the police constituted an "occupying army," then liberating the ghetto from their grip would require an equal magnitude of force and sacrifice.

Samb's performance recalled Newton, but it did not copy him. Samb's grey beard and locks contrasted sharply with Newton's clean-shaven, youthful appearance. And where Newton sits with his feet firmly planted, meeting his onlookers with a militant, unflinching gaze, Samb's legs were crossed and his countenance was more introspective, his eyes sullen. He was the old man who has outlived the revolution, or maybe a ghost. We worship long-dead heroes because they are no longer a part of the difficult tug and pull of historical forces that make our own world. Samb presented us with the revolutionary in the glass case—perhaps a reference to the macabre practice of embalming state socialism's founders in perpetuity. The revolutionary is entombed, walled off from our own cultural and social world, no longer a part of our sense of living political possibilities.

Sitting on the edge of some of Chicago's most impoverished and violent neighborhoods, the abandoned storefront itself signals death—yet another casualty in the cycles of divestment, real estate speculation, and displacement afflicting central cities across the United States. Not long into Samb's performance, these looming urban realities interrupted the celebration, after a scuffle broke out between groups of young men assembled in an upstairs art gallery for the opening reception. Within minutes, police cruisers careened onto the sidewalk, flak-jacketed officers rushed inside to quell the disturbance, and many attendees, some of them Panther veterans, were left shaking their heads in disbelief. In its juxtaposition of movement nostalgia and lingering urban misery, Samb's performance inspired revival, the revolutionary apparition staring back once again from a blighted corner of the ghetto.

The slogan "Black Lives Matter" rose to prominence the summer before Samb's storefront performance. Three black feminist activists created the Twitter hashtag after the 2012 vigilante killing of Trayvon Martin, an unarmed black teen in Sanford, Florida. Over the next few years, thousands embraced the slogan, protesting sporting events, staging die-ins on sidewalks, occupying public offices, and shutting down highways. Such actions forced the undeserved deaths of black civilians into the public conscience and created a crisis of legitimacy for the dominant approaches to urban policing. Although struggles against policing have a much longer lineage, the current renewal of anti-racist organizing crystallized out of discrete historical conjunctures—the comprehensive surveillance of society through private and public security video feeds and smartphone cameras, the advent of social media networks that connect millions of users worldwide and enable instantaneous circulation of information, the hollowing out of the social welfare state and further deterioration of inner-city life in the wake of the subprime mortgage crisis and ensuing recession, and the debates over post-racialism that accompanied the Obama presidency.

Despite the frequency and power of mass demonstrations, we are no closer to achieving concrete, substantive reform that might curtail police violence and ensure greater democratic accountability. To be frank, if we are going to end this crisis and achieve genuine public safety and peace, the current struggles must grow beyond street demonstrations to build popular consensus and effective power. The road to reaching those ends is currently blocked. Part of the problem resides in the prevailing nostalgia for Black Power militancy and the continued pursuit of modes of black ethnic politics. Such nostalgia is underwritten by the vindicationist posture of recent scholarly writing on the subject and is abetted by the digital afterlife of movement imagery, which preserves the most emotionally impactful elements of the movement but is consumed in ways that forget Black Power's historical origins and intrinsic limitations.

At the heart of contemporary organizing is the notion of black exceptionalism. Contemporary Black Lives Matter activists and supporters insist on the uniqueness of the black predicament and on the need for race-specific remedies. "Black Lives Matter is an ideological and political intervention in a world where black lives are systematically and intentionally targeted for demise," Black Lives Matter co-founder

Alicia Garza explains. "It is an affirmation of Black folks' contributions to this society, our humanity and our resistance in the face of deadly oppression."[1] "When we say Black Lives Matter," Garza continues, "we are talking about the ways in which Black people are deprived of our basic human rights and dignity. It is an acknowledgement [that] Black poverty and genocide [are] state violence." This essay takes aim at this notion of black exceptionalism and lays out its origins and limits as an analysis of hyperpolicing and, more generally, as an effective political orientation capable of building the popular power needed to end the policing crisis.

We begin by revisiting the social and ideological roots of black ethnic politics as we know it. Black Power unfolded within a context of class fragmentation; the decline of the left labor militancy of the Depression, wartime, and the post–World War II years; and the transformation of metropolitan space after the 1949 Housing Act, which produced suburban homeownership and upward mobility for many whites and inner-city ghettoization and exploitation for the black poor. The combination of shifting urban demography, rising black political efficacy created by the Southern civil rights/desegregation campaigns, and the liberal statecraft of Lyndon B. Johnson's administration framed the turn to Black Power and associated demands for black control of political and economic institutions. In the Black Power era, we can see the origins of contemporary hyper-ghettoization and intensive policing of the black poor as well as the ascendancy of post-segregation patron-client relations between an expanding black professional-managerial class and the mainstream parties, corporations, and private foundations. This evolution of Black Power as an elite-driven ethnic politics ultimately negated and transcended the revolutionary potential implied in calls for black self-determination and socialist revolution. If you believe that the "Movement for Black Lives" is the second coming of Black Power, this historical process may give us some sense of where it is going.

The notion of black ethnic politics remains at the heart of Black Lives Matter protests and falsely equates racial identity with political constituency. "Black Power" and "Black Lives Matter" as political slogans are rooted in racial standpoint epistemology—that is, the notion that, by virtue of the common experience of racism, African Americans possess territorial ways of knowing the world and, by extension, deeply shared political interests. This commonsensical view is a mystification that elides the differing and conflicting material interests and ideological positions that animate black political life in real time and space.

The second part of this essay examines these differences and conflicts in light of the celebrated release of the *Vision for Black Lives* agenda, which contains a set of progressive policy demands but is guided by the counterproductive assumptions of black unity politics, which have historically facilitated elite brokerage dynamics rather than building effective counter-power. Just as readily as it can be used to advance left social justice demands, the "Black Lives Matter" slogan can—and on occasion already has—become a vehicle for entrepreneurial branding and courting philanthropic foundations. Similarly, it can express bourgeois interests (e.g., "Black

Wealth Matters") and education privatization agendas just as easily as it can express working-class interests and the promotion of public education.

The third section of this essay develops a critique of black exceptionalism, the central premise of contemporary discussions of inequality and campaigns against police violence. The current policing crisis and carceral state are not a reincarnation of the Jim Crow regime. They are, rather, core features of post–welfare state capitalism, where punitive strategies for managing social inequality have replaced benevolent welfare state interventions and where managing the surplus population has become a key function of law enforcement and the prison system. Allusions to a "New Jim Crow" racism continue to have moral sway in some corners and retain the capacity to mobilize citizens in large numbers, but the analysis that underpins them is inadequate to provide the foundations for building left politics. If the current struggles are to become an aggregate force powerful enough to win concrete gains in terms of social justice, a critical first step is for activists to abandon this tendency to substitute analogy for analysis. The premise of black exceptionalism obscures contemporary social realities and actual political alignments, and forestalls honest conversations about the real class interests dominating today's neoliberal urban landscape.

The Roots of Black Ethnic Politics

The familiar leftist lore of Black Power is one of a heroic movement, a time when black denizens rose up in insurrection against imperialism on foreign shores and in the heart of the nation's cities, a movement where revolutionary dreams of black liberation were crushed by state repression. The broad outlines of this story are true, but the history of Black Power is more complex. The origins of Black Power rest in the unique social and demographic realities of black urban life after World War II and, equally, in the social consequences and limits of the Second Reconstruction: liberal policy reforms produced by the interplay of civil rights movement pressure and the presidential administration of Lyndon B. Johnson, which abolished legal segregation in the South and integrated blacks as consumer-citizens.

Black mass migration after World War II and the segregative dynamics of housing policy under the Harry Truman presidency created the social preconditions for this era of reform and black urban empowerment. A manifestation of real estate industry power, the 1949 Housing Act set in motion the radical spatial transformation of American cities, earmarking funds for urban renewal and public housing construction and creating federally insured mortgages for suburban single-family-home purchases—measures that combined to produce the urban-suburban wealth inequality that would define American public life for more than a half century.

Housing discrimination and ethnic-enclave settlement patterns limited most blacks to the same proximal urban neighborhoods, even though those black ghettos were internally stratified along class lines, with the black middle class occupying better, safer housing stock.[2] Postwar urban renewal further concretized this residential apartheid, as federal interstate highways and other massive public projects bisected black neighborhoods, dispersing residents, destroying the urban fabric, devaluing adjacent property, and often serving as physical walls dividing black areas from those of other ethnicities. Slum clearance and the construction of tower block housing, which were widely supported by downtown commercial interests and social reformers, momentarily improved the environs of those previously relegated to dangerous, unsanitary tenement conditions, but these developments were in effect a form of vertical ghettoization.

During the same epoch, the peacetime industrial demobilization undermined many black workers' attempts to find gainful employment and earn a living wage. Given their status as newcomers in many industries, they were among the first to be handed pink slips during cyclical downturns. The relocation of manufacturing facilities from city centers to suburban greenfields and the ongoing adoption of labor-saving production technology further diminished job prospects for less skilled and less educated black urban newcomers. Chrysler autoworker James Boggs was among the first black intellectuals to offer a critical left perspective of industrial automation, cybernetics, and their political implications within and beyond the factory gates.[3] Boggs referred to the black men he increasingly saw standing idle on Detroit street corners as "outsiders," "expendables," and "untouchables," those who were among the first to experience technological obsolescence and had little hope of industrial integration. This figure of black unemployed youth during the late fifties and early sixties should have served as a miner's canary, a harbinger of the precarious conditions produced by labor arbitrage and technology-intensive production, as well as plain and simple prolonged recession and rationalization of the work force by way of speedup. But their plight was drowned out in the high tide of postwar economic prosperity during the sixties and early seventies; in liberal circles, their condition was explained in a manner that disconnected the black urban poor from the rest of the working class. Black Power militants would speak directly to these conditions of unemployment and ghetto isolation, but their movement did not only emerge from below in response to the oppressive conditions facing the ghetto/black urban population, as is commonly asserted. Rather, it was also encouraged by liberal statecraft from above.

Historians of the Black Power era tend to neglect the relationship between its popular manifestations and Johnson's War on Poverty initiative. This is an unfortunate oversight that may stem in part from the desire of some scholars to valorize black self-activity. But the resulting interpretive bias has no doubt stalled the development of analyses that fully appreciate the complex origins and built-in limitations of Black Power as a sociopolitical phenomenon. Even before "Black Power" became a popular slogan, one that was simultaneously edifying to many blacks who desired real self-determination and frightening to some whites who associated it with violent retribution, liberals in the Johnson White House were retailing their own version of black empowerment: one that addressed class inequality, but in a language of ethno-cultural exceptionalism.

Johnson's assistant secretary of labor, Daniel Patrick Moynihan, took the lead in this regard, authoring his report *The Negro Family: The Case for National Action* to build support for progressive legislation addressing urban poverty. In his 1965 Howard University commencement address, Johnson best summed up the core assumption of the Moynihan Report when he asserted, "Negro poverty is not white poverty."[4] Working under this notion of Negro exceptionalism, Moynihan argued that black poverty amid white prosperity was due to a combination of institutional racism and the alleged cultural pathology of the black poor themselves. This "culture of poverty" sentiment was widely embraced by Moynihan's contemporaries, including such diverse figures as anthropologist Oscar Lewis, sociologist Kenneth Clark, and even democratic socialist Michael Harrington.[5] Yet some Black Power elements would also accept this culturalist argument, even if their politics were more radical—recall the Black Panthers' formative position on the lumpenproletariat, which cast this substratum as dysfunctional but potentially revolutionary. This Cold War turn toward cultural explanations of minority poverty within the liberal wing of the New Deal coalition marked a rejection of the class-centered politics that had defined both the labor militancy of the interwar period and the political orientation of the postwar civil rights movement.

The shifting terrain of working-class consciousness and politics within American life during the sixties was the direct result of decades-long interrelated processes. Progressive labor activism was undermined in part by the rise in wages and benefits that resulted from the high levels of investment and employment that came with the long postwar boom, and that provided the basis for the expansion of a normative middle-class ideal of homeownership and leisure consumption. It was tamed, too, by the anti-communist witch hunts that targeted unions, left parties, civil rights organizations, and Hollywood. Reflecting the balance of class forces during the 1930s, the New Deal was a tangible expression of the interests of particular blocs of capital as well as the outcome of constraints that workers and popular movements imposed on capitalism.[6] The National Recovery Administration sought to address the capitalist contradictions that led to the 1929 stock market crash and ensuing crisis, the weak regulation of the financial markets, and the surplus absorption problem stemming from the lack of effective demand for manufactured goods. The 1935 Wagner Act's formal recognition of the right to organize was intended to stabilize labor-management relations and provide a means for resolving disputes in a manner that did not disrupt production and capital flows. This legislation responded to the massive pressure from below that came with the explosion of labor militancy that culminated in three great urban general strikes in 1934. Those strikes had the effect of stimulating a wave of shop floor organizing led by the Congress of Industrial Organizations (CIO), which was founded in 1935 as a breakaway from the more conservative, craft-oriented American Federation of Labor (AFL). Through militant tactics and vigorous organizing, the CIO succeeded in unionizing workers in factories, steel mills, shipyards, docks, and packinghouses throughout the United States and Canada. In response to a wave of CIO-led strikes after the war, Congress passed the 1947 Taft-Hartley Act, which criminalized solidarity and the general strike, signaling the effective end of the era of CIO militancy—the organization was reunited with the AFL in 1955—and ushering in a period of mostly business-centered labor relations.[7]

Contrary to the popular view of the fifties as an era of mass quiescence, labor unrest continued through the decade, but the expansion of the consumer society and the growth of suburbia weakened progressive unionism. The hearts and minds of many American workers were won over to capitalist growth imperatives through the promise of rising wages, spacious tract housing, the personal mobility of automobile culture, and the enlarged leisure industries reflected in television, drive-in theaters, and shopping malls. The pastoral and technological comforts of suburbia reminded Americans of capitalism's virtues, while active state repression prescribed clear social consequences to those who dared openly criticize the system's contradictions and faults.

Beginning with the Palmer Raids of 1919 and 1920, where socialists and anarchists were rounded up, arrested and deported, the US state and local police took a more prominent role in repressing workplace organizing. With the creation of the Federal Bureau of Investigation, the national state consolidated, enlarged, and rationalized the policing of working-class militancy that in earlier moments of class struggle had been undertaken by Pinkerton saboteurs and hired guns. Reliance on repressive forces at the state and local level played an important part in limiting the impact of workers' mass militancy in the early New Deal years. After World War II and as US–Soviet tensions sharpened with the instigation of Truman, the ruling class undertook a concerted campaign to extinguish Communist influence within domestic trade unions. The campaign against the radical left, led by the House Un-American Activities Committee, blacklisted and harassed scores of citizens suspected of Communist sympathy and took an obsessive interest in rooting out reds in the Screen Actors Guild, given the enlarged role of television and movies in shaping American leisure culture, romantic sentiments, and political dispositions.

McCarthyism was especially consequential for the struggle to defeat Jim Crow, since the Communist Party (CP) had played a pivotal role in addressing the "Negro question" during the interwar period through the Scottsboro Boys trials, the formation of the National Negro Congress (NNC), and organizing black sharecroppers in the Deep South. Black and white leftists with ties to the CP and the union movement also built powerful support networks and activist training programs, such the Highlander Folk School. Red-baiting destroyed careers and reputations, bred suspicion and distrust within the left, and had a chilling effect on the postwar civil rights movement, bolstering liberal integration as the most viable option for black emancipation within the Cold War context. Liberal anti-racism found traction in this context of defeated labor militancy, one where open class analysis and commitment to socialist revolution often spelled financial and personal ruin for those who dared stray from the emergent Cold War rules of acceptable political discourse.

In his analysis of how liberals like Moynihan came to separate race and class, historian Touré Reed reminds us that during the interwar period, through World War II, and well after, organizing based on class was widely accepted as an effective way for blacks to amass power and secure economic gains—specifically participation in the dynamic labor movement of the era. Civil rights leaders like A. Philip Randolph of the Brotherhood of Sleeping Car Porters union and the wartime March on Washington Movement, Lester Granger of the National Urban League, Walter White of the National Association for the Advancement of Colored People (NAACP), and John P. Davis of the NNC all "frequently argued that precisely because most blacks were working class, racial equality could only be achieved through a combination of anti-discrimination policies and social-democratic economic policies."[8] Some latter-day Black Lives Matter activists, Reed notes, might well reject such a position, which was commonly held by labor and civil rights veterans during the sixties, as "vulgar class reductionis[m]." Although he would increasingly embrace a politics of insider negotiation during the sixties, veteran activist Bayard Rustin insisted that black progress could only be achieved through the development of broad, interracial coalitions dedicated to social democracy, a position that drew the ire of some Black Power radicals.[9] The social democratic perspective touted by Randolph, Rustin, and others was clearly expressed in their 1966 *Freedom Budget* and actually continued to resonate throughout the decade—perhaps most famously in the 1963 March on Washington but also, for example, in the Memphis sanitation workers' strike actively supported by Martin Luther King Jr. But this political tendency was ultimately eclipsed by the liberal Democratic focus on racial discrimination and the culture of poverty as distinct problems, separate from the labor-management accord, unionization, and matters of political economy.[10]

The liberal decoupling of race and class supplanted more radical versions of working-class left politics, with far-reaching political consequences, operating now as a form of common sense. During the sixties, this view of Negro exceptionalism filled the vacuum left by interwar labor militancy. It gained traction with the deepening physical separation of black and white workers, which came with the spatial transformation of cities that sent white workers and much industry to the suburbs and left blacks in the urban ghettos. Moreover, by framing the problem of black poverty in terms of discrimination and alleged cultural pathology, liberals, who were now strongly allied with capital, systematically failed to address structural unemployment and the prevalence of nonunion, unprotected employment, two of the root causes of durable poverty among urban blacks. Liberal anti-poverty efforts were limited, as many black activists readily pointed out at the time. Unlike the New Deal legislation, which expanded collective bargaining rights and public works, the Johnson administration's Great Society legislation took care not to upset the lucrative patronage relations between the federal government and private contractors in the construction and defense sectors, central motors of the postwar economic boom. The Great Society was limited in its capacity to end black urban poverty but powerful in terms of its political impact, as it subsidized and legitimated the expansion of a post-segregation black political elite.

The Johnson administration oversaw a period of domestic social reform that restored black civil rights and went a step further in providing various forms of targeted aid to address racial and urban inequality. Historian Kent Germany examines how War on Poverty reforms were implemented in New Orleans and their consequences for the growth of the black professional-managerial class there. He characterizes the War on Poverty approach as a soft state, "a loose set of short-term political and bureaucratic arrangements that linked together federal bureaucracies, neighborhood groups, nonprofit organizations, semipublic political organizations, social agencies, and, primarily after 1970, local government" to distribute federal funding to predominantly black neighborhoods.[11] The Community Action Program, Volunteers in Service to America (VISTA), Head Start, and Job Corps, as well as the 1966 Demonstration Cities legislation, were especially supportive of Black Power's genesis and evolution.

These various programs of the War on Poverty encouraged black political incorporation along the established lines of ethnic patron-clientelism and nurtured a discrete form of bourgeois class politics, one that mobilized and rewarded the most articulate elements of urban communities of color. The Community Action Program sought the "maximum feasible participation" of the urban black and brown poor in devising solutions to their collective plight. The result was a form of ethnic empowerment that eventually enabled black constituencies to wrest control from white ethnic-dominated governments in many cities, but that also averted a working class–centered politics by institutionalizing the view that racial identity and political constituency were synonymous.

As it turned out, Black Power militancy and the managerial logic of the Great Society were symbiotic. Figures as diverse as Newark mayor Kenneth Gibson and Black Panther Party co-founder Bobby Seale participated in and led anti-poverty programs. The Community Action Agencies provided established black leadership, neighborhood activists, and aspiring politicos with access, resources, and socialization into the world of local public administration. Moynihan later claimed that "the most important long-run impact" of the Community Action Program was the "formation of an urban Negro leadership echelon at just the time when the Negro masses and other minorities were verging toward extensive commitments to urban politics." Recalling the quintessential political machine of Gilded Age New York, Moynihan concluded that "Tammany at its best (or worse) would have envied the political apprenticeship provided the neighborhood coordinators of the anti-poverty programs."[12] Although Black Power evocations of Third World revolution and armed struggle carried an air of militancy, the real and imagined threat posed by Black Power activists helped to enhance the leverage of more moderate leadership elements, facilitating integration and patronage linkages that delivered to them urban political control and expanded the ranks of the black professional-managerial stratum. The threat of black militancy, either in the form of armed Panther patrols or the phantom black sniper evoked by public authorities amid urban rioting, facilitated elite brokerage dynamics and political integration. Instead of abolishing the conditions of structural unemployment, disinvestment, and hyper-segregation that increasingly defined the inner city, Black Power delivered official recognition and elite representation.

Two of the most influential texts of the period, Harold Cruse's *The Crisis of the Negro Intellectual* and Stokely Carmichael and Charles V. Hamilton's *Black Power: The Politics of Liberation in America*, both published in 1967, naturalized the rise of Black Power as entailing the black electoral takeover of urban politics by interpreting it in terms of the so-called ethnic framework, which saw the integration of successive waves of immigrants into American life by way of city government and its fruits.[13] In his opening chapter, "Individualism and the Open Society," Cruse, implicitly adopting a liberal pluralist perspective, argued that American society was essentially organized through various social groups, with "ethnic blocs" being the most powerful.[14] He claimed that civil rights were a meaningless abstraction outside of the formal, influential political groups that could give them material and practical force. Following this logic, blacks possessed few rights, according to Cruse, because black leadership had failed to act in the nationalistic manner historically pursued by other ethnic groups. Carmichael and Hamilton concluded, in a similar vein, that "group solidarity is necessary before a group can operate effectively from a bargaining position of strength in a pluralistic society."[15] Many argue that the Black Panther Party for Self-Defense represented a more revolutionary alternative to this more conservative black ethnic politics, and to a considerable extent it did. But it must be pointed out that the embrace by some Panthers and other black radical organizations of the colonial analogy and other versions of black exceptionalism abided the same logics.

Organizations like the Black Panther Party fought against police violence, hunger, and slum landlords, and mobilized local communities in solidarity with Third World liberation struggles. Creative intellectuals, artists, and musicians affiliated with the Black Arts Movement also unleashed a short-lived urban renaissance in which local black communities dreamed of a world where ghettos were seen not as zones to be escaped and abandoned, but as spaces that might be reborn, giving rise to a popular democratic urbanism not possible under the segregation and exploitation most blacks endured. Unlike the civil rights movement, however, which over the course of decades amassed the resources and popular support needed to wage a successful fight to defeat Jim Crow segregation, Black Power's radical tendencies attained mass resonance but never achieved truly national popular support for the revolutionary projects they advocated.

This crucial distinction between movement notoriety and actual popular power is conflated within the scholarship and folklore of Black Power.[16] Certainly, during the sixties and seventies, some whites supported the Panthers during their highly publicized court cases; many also funded the legal defense of jailed Panthers, because such imprisonment was on false grounds and threatened the rule of law and judicial due process. Others rallied alongside Panther cadre in opposition to the Vietnam War or supported specific initiatives, like their survival programs. But how many middle-class or working-class Americans fully embraced the party's call for socialist revolution, as they had the civil rights movement? And was this perspective, one inflected with Third Worldism and allusions to armed struggle, at all suited to the affluent, advanced industrial society in which it was propagated? These are questions that latter-day historians and fans of the Black Power movement have, for the most part, failed to answer or even to pose.

The interplay of patronage, solidarity, and surrogacy that defined relations between Black Power radicals and New Leftists obscured the deeper challenges that pervasive anti-communism and the intimate relation between commercial Keynesianism, local economic growth, and middle-class living standards and cultural expectations all posed for the development of a left revolutionary politics during this period. Mass demonstrations, urban rebellions, police repression, and assassinations signaled a crisis of legitimacy for the nation's governing institutions and gave the impression of imminent revolution, but these events and the rhetorical excesses of the age also concealed the depth of social cleavages, the resiliency and unity of the ruling class, and the extent of conservative political commitments within the broader populace. In this context, black revolution was political theater for too many white Americans, rather than a project that connected effectively with their anxieties, daily struggles, and desires.

The failure to build powerful working-class solidarity during this particular historical juncture, of course, does not fall solely on the shoulders of Black Power radicals, who were often more courageous than any other political element in naming the system's failures and advancing a critique of imperial power, even under the threat of repression and death. If Black Power radicals tended to see urban black life as fundamentally distinct from that of whites, organized labor failed in the same regard, proving to be either unable or unwilling to invest in both cross-sectoral and intercommunity organizing—in other words, organizing the working class as a class *for itself*. This was, of course, a legacy of Taft-Hartley and the turn to K Street–oriented unionism, but it was an especially acute problem during the seventies and eighties, when the ruling class set about organizing to break the power of unions and roll back redistributive social policy.

Writing at the dawn of the Nixon era, Bay Area–based writer and activist Robert Allen was especially perceptive in grasping the nascent political realignments occurring underneath the pronouncement of the most militant demands of Black Power, and the role that the black professional-managerial class would play in the emerging political-economic order. Allen concluded that

> the white corporate elite has found an ally in the black bourgeoisie, the new, militant black middle class which became a significant social force following World War II.

> The members of this class consist of black professionals, technicians, executives, professors, government workers, etc . . . Like the black masses, they denounced the old black elite of Tomming preachers, teachers, and business-men-politicians . . . The new black elite seeks to overthrow and take the place of this old elite.[17]

To accomplish this, Allen continued, "it has forged an informal alliance with the corporate forces which run white (and black) America."[18] Limited but significant political integration had changed the face of public leadership in most American cities, with some having elected successive black-led governing regimes. In retrospect, the Black Power movement was a transitional stage where black popular discontent diversified the nation's governing class.

The process of black Democratic Party incorporation was already under way but still in flux when Johnson signed omnibus civil rights reforms and initiated the political recruitment strategies of the War on Poverty. The previous generation of black political elites like Chicago's William L. Dawson and Archibald Carey Jr., who began their political careers before World War II, had done so in the "party of Lincoln." A few, like Massachusetts senator Edward Brooke, remained in the Republican ranks even as the Southern desegregation campaigns gave way to the demand for Black Power. Already during the sixties, some black Democrats were being elected in those cities where the postwar migration had expanded the black population into a coveted voting bloc, and this first generation of black elected leadership remained largely

committed to protecting the gains of the civil rights movement and what remained of the social welfare state.

During the seventies and eighties, many black-led city
regimes actually succeeded in reducing incidences of police
brutality against black citizens.[19] But that success in regulating police misconduct was short-lived, produced by the
contingency of liberal black political leadership, integrating
police departments, and the presence of activist black publics.
This period of reform was largely brought to an end with the
onset of the Reagan years, which witnessed the escalation of
the War on Drugs, the horrifying rates of drug-related and
gang violence that accompanied the crack epidemic, and the
concomitant expansion of the carceral state. The achieve-
ments of the brief era of black-led police reform should
remind us of the possibility of effective public remedy, but
also of the limitations of Black Power. The efforts of black
mayors and city council majorities to curb police violence in
the seventies and eighties were overrun by national- and
state-level forces that sought to manage growing inequality
and impoverishment through incarceration; black politicians
and constituencies who supported the War on Drugs were
instrumental in legitimating and advancing those efforts. The
turn to neoliberalism within the Democratic Party and the
parallel collapse of the New Deal coalition have since transformed black political life, rendering appeals to big-tent race
unity and the pursuit of traditional racial redress anachronistic. Such changes have facilitated the rise of a new black urban
political leadership that has been consolidating its power
through forging ever more extensive commitments to

Democratic Party neoliberalism. This is the historical terrain of the Movement for Black Lives: one where reform is possible, but the forces arrayed in support of the carceral state cannot be explained in black and white.

The Movement for Black Lives and the Neoliberal Landscape

The contemporary Movement for Black Lives is a diverse phenomenon—horizontal, decentralized, and driven by organizations like Black Lives Matter, the Dream Defenders, the Black Youth Project 100, Assata's Daughters, Freedom, Inc., Southerners on New Ground, Leaders of a Beautiful Struggle, and dozens of other youth groups, black student unions, and community-based organizations. Contemporary protests have found broad support among liberals, black nationalists, socialists, clergy, politicians, and civil liberties advocates. More than their predecessors, the activists now leading the fight against police and vigilante violence have foregrounded feminist and queer-affirming perspectives, demanding a culture of respect and participation to redress the historical dominance of civil rights and black political activism by heterosexual, male, and often religious leadership. As these struggles have grown in size and in their capacity to disrupt the normal order, like all social struggles they have developed their own subculture, with dedicated protest chants, memes, songs, and tactical styles and with youth activists sometimes referring to themselves as the new vanguard. As with the turn to Afrocentricism and black nationalist–inflected rap music during the waning years of the Reagan-Bush era, the aesthetic politics of Black Power militancy have been resurrected, complete with clenched-fist salutes; talk of black consciousness, self-help, and black love; and an insistence that race unity is a prerequisite for effective political action.

The 2016 *Vision for Black Lives* agenda is a platform containing a battery of demands that connect police violence to broader matters of inequality. It reflects the real potential of the Black Lives Matter tendency but also the extent to which its activism remains mired in unhelpful assumptions about the liberal democratic political process. The *Vision* agenda was released by activists in the aftermath of national protests of the police killings of Alton Sterling in Baton Rouge, Louisiana, and Philando Castile near St. Paul, Minnesota. The agenda also appeared after two black snipers killed police officers en masse in two separate incidents, after which Black Lives Matter protestors faced a wave of denunciation by "Blue Lives Matter" reactionaries. The agenda's preamble boldly declares, "Black humanity and dignity requires black political will and power . . . We are a collective that centers on and is rooted in Black communities, but we recognize we have a shared struggle with all oppressed people; collective liberation will be a product of all of our work."[20]

The *Vision for Black Lives* agenda contains an impressive list of left policy planks such as universal basic income, demilitarization of policing, an end to money bail, decriminalization of sex work and drugs, strengthening collective bargaining, and building a cooperative economy. If ever realized, it would go a long way toward creating a more just and civilized society. Some have cheered the agenda's release as a major step toward consolidating power and as a marked departure from the kind of expressive politics that defined Occupy Wall Street, where anarcho-liberal political tendencies were openly hostile to the idea of making demands on the state. I agree with these observations in part, but the agenda and its underlying political assumptions nonetheless inherit many of the problems of Black Power politics and, quite honestly, fail to learn from the last half century of black political development.

Not enough of those who have championed the agenda have critically reflected on the problems surrounding the pursuit of similar black agendas historically. Historian Robin D.G. Kelley praises the agenda as "less a political platform than a plan for ending structural racism, saving the planet and transforming the entire nation—not just black lives."[21] Although he is surely aware of the fate of comparable agenda-setting efforts since the Black Power era, Kelley does not pause to consider the patent limitations of this brand of identity politics and the glaring fact that, even if the black population achieved broad unity around this agenda, which is unlikely, that would not be enough to compel city councils, state legislatures, or Congress to pass any of its demands. Despite its progressive aspirations, the *Vision* agenda will likely succumb to the same problems as those produced during the Black Power movement because it proceeds from the specious view that effective politics should be built on the grounds of ethnic affinity rather than discrete political interests.

A comparable agenda was produced by participants at the 1972 National Black Political Convention in Gary, Indiana. Numbering in the thousands, that delegation was much larger, more politically integrated, and more broadly representative of the black population than the various organizations that produced the recent *Vision* agenda. And unlike today, when neoliberal politics unites both parties on matters of social policy, international trade, and economic development, at the time of the Gary Convention, the US Congress and the Democratic Party were still largely comprised of New Deal liberals and progressive urban politicians who broadly accepted the utility of state power to address racial discrimination and inequality. Despite this more favorable context and the actual political entrée and influence of the Gary delegates, little from their 1972 agenda ever materialized as local or national policy. Even before its closing gavel sounded, the convention delegation was rocked by defections over platform planks that supported Palestinian self-determination and an end to busing as a strategy for achieving school integration. Rather than developing into a means of maintaining black unity and collective power as organizers had hoped, competing groups and individuals marshaled the convention's national media exposure as means for bargaining with the mainstream parties.

The *Vision for Black Lives* agenda is not backed by the same kind of cadre of activists and veteran politicos who produced the 1972 Gary agenda. Those who crafted the *Vision* agenda are younger and less politically integrated, and some are openly suspicious of conventional partisan politics.

It remains to be seen whether the Movement for Black Lives can develop a viable political approach capable of leveraging mass demonstrations into actual policy outcomes. In fact, when pressed to deal with this sort of basic tactical and strategic political question, some supporters dismiss them as antiquated and reformist. Yet without addressing these questions, producing a list of demands, no matter how visionary, will do little to end the current crisis and abolish poverty and racial inequality.

There are moments when the *Vision* agenda's framing of specific issues and policy proposals departs from the universal spirit of the 1972 Gary agenda and similar agendas produced during the sixties, like the 1966 *Freedom Budget*. A good illustration of this is where the *Vision* agenda turns to matters of political economy. In addition to voicing support for stronger workers' rights and protections, progressive taxation, and opposition to the Trans-Pacific Partnership trade bill, the agenda's economic justice section calls for "federal and state job programs that specifically target the most economically marginalized Black people, and compensation for those involved in the care economy."[22] But given the decades of backlash against means-tested social policy, it would seem that there would be some consideration of how to build popular support beyond the black population in our current political context. This would seem to require a willingness to push for universal public works projects along the lines of the Civilian Conservation Corps—meaning a program that would be publicly financed, publicly managed, and subject to anti-discrimination regulation. The most progressive planks contained within the *Vision for Black Lives* agenda cannot be achieved without popular support and majority coalitions, but this version of identity politics, which aims high but remains narrowly committed to the ethnic paradigm, runs counter to those ends.

With some exceptions, the Movement for Black Lives more generally is guided by an understanding of political life that sees racial affinity as synonymous with constituency. This much is clear when the authors of the *Vision* agenda declare, "We have created this platform to articulate and support the ambitions and work of Black people. We also seek to intervene in the current political climate and assert a clear vision, particularly for those who claim to be our allies, of the world we want them to help us create." This passage assumes a rather simplistic view of black people's ambitions and interests and draws a false dividing line between the interests of blacks and nonblacks—"those who claim to be our allies." Clearly descendant from Black Power thinking, this statement presumes a commonality of interests among blacks and claims authority to speak on behalf of those interests with little sense of irony. Broad acceptance of the myth of a corporate black body politic authorizes the very elite brokerage dynamics that many younger activists dislike about established civil rights organizations.

Despite the insistence of some supporters that there is a progressive pro-working-class politics at the heart of Black Lives Matter activism, the rapture of "unapologetic blackness" and the ethnic politics that imbues various programmatic efforts will continue to lead away from the kind of cosmopolitan, popular political work that is needed to end the policing crisis. There are, of course, different ideological tendencies operating within the Movement for Black Lives: radical, progressive, bourgeois and reactionary. The spats between Black Lives Matter's founders and those who sought to use the hashtag without their permission reflected a proprietary sensibility more suited to product branding and entrepreneurship than to popular social struggle. If the Gary Convention experience is the model here, then what we might expect is the fracturing of the Movement for Black Lives into different brokerage camps, each claiming to represent the "black community" more effectively than the other but none capable of amassing the counterpower necessary to have a lasting political impact.

Black Lives Matter co-founder Patrisse Cullors gives a sense of this problem when she says that she will continue to work with black neoliberals because of their common racial affinity. "That I don't agree with neoliberalism doesn't encourage me to launch an online assault against those who do. We can, in fact, agree to disagree. We can have a healthy debate. We can show up for one another as Black folks inside of this movement in ways that don't isolate, terrorize, and shame people—something I've experienced firsthand."[23] Cullors is right when she asserts that political work involves building bonds of trust and a willingness to respect different opinions. But such work is best undertaken outside the echo chambers of social media, which most often encourage irresponsible rhetoric, amplify identitarian assumptions, and suffocate public-spiritedness. Cullors mistakes the core basis of political life, however.

Sustained political work is held together by shared historical interests, especially those that connect to our daily lives and felt needs, not sentimental "ties of blood."

Cullors and many other activists embrace the Black Power premise of the necessity of black unity, once expressed in phrases like "operational unity" and "unity without uniformity" and in familial metaphors about "not airing dirty laundry" and settling disputes "in-house." The problem with this sentiment is that it reduces the divergent political interests animating black life at any given historical moment to happenstance, external manipulation, or superficial grievance. As well, this call for black unity is always underwritten by the fiction that other groups have advanced through the ethnic paradigm, a view that is patently ahistorical and neglects the role of interracial alliances in creating a more democratic, just society. This line of thinking always assumes that there is something underneath it all that binds black people together politically, but that reasoning must always rely on some notion of racial essentialism and a suspension of any honest analysis of black political life as it exists.

Just as there were black elites poised to advance a version of Black Power as black capitalism and patron-clientelism, similar forces exist within the contemporary Movement for Black Lives. One schism that has grown more pronounced is between those who support privatizing education and others who view charter schools and market-oriented reforms as attempts to break teachers' unions and diminish accountability, universal access, and equality in public schools. Ferguson activists Johnetta Elzie, DeRay Mckesson, and Brittany

Packnett have allied themselves with Teach for America, an education privatization group that supplies nonunion, low-wage, and inexperienced teachers to urban school districts. Pro-charter advocate and St. Paul activist Rashad Anthony Turner renounced Black Lives Matter after national organizers called for a moratorium on charter schools.[24] When we look at local conflicts over education, such as those over the school privatization efforts undertaken by deposed DC mayor Adrian Fenty and education-reform mercenary Michelle Rhee, the formation of the New Orleans Recovery School District, or the 2012 Chicago Teachers Union strike and Mayor Rahm Emanuel's subsequent neighborhood school closures and layoffs, we find blacks on both sides. In the fight to defend and improve public education, there is no unified "black interest" as such. In these instances, the assumptions of common racial interests run headlong into lived black politics and the diverse and conflicting constituencies operating within the black population at any given historical moment.

The Problem with Black Exceptionalism

The Movement for Black Lives expresses black angst amid economic recession, home foreclosures and evictions, dwindling public relief, intense police violence, and prevailing social meanness, but the anti-racist frame is inadequate for explaining the complex sources of this mass unease. We need to clarify the fundamental causes of contemporary inequality and the policing crisis, as well as the role of multicultural political elites and the humanitarian-corporate complex in advancing the neoliberal project. To this end, a more critical approach to localized power and the actuality of racial representation might help activists better anticipate the forces and processes that cajoled and contained the 2015 mass protests in Baltimore and Chicago. In both these places, token firings, suspensions, and indictments of police, the dissipation of popular energy by nonprofits, and the opportunistic maneuvers of both black and white political elites of various stripes had the combined effect of deflecting mass pressure and preserving the status quo.[25] Liberal anti-racism, with its core assumption of black exceptionalism, helps enable these social management dynamics because it overlooks the integrated nature of contemporary governance in many American cities and the crucial role that black elites can play in legitimating the current neoliberal order.

The hegemony of liberal anti-racism stems from how well it stands in for an analysis of capitalist class relations. The spatial-economic reorganization of American cities after the Second World War—the creation of inner-city black public housing and suburban white single-family homes—entrenched black and white as the symbolic referents of class inequality in American public debate. Many whites who had endured tremendous hardship during the Great Depression improved their material condition by way of the historic postwar economic boom and the ensuing birth of the consumer republic, which for the first time made homeownership, quality education, job opportunities, and middle-class lifestyles available to them. During the same period, blacks were nominally integrated into the consumer society through civil rights pressure, anti-discrimination legislation and the arrival of black urban regimes that created a path to the middle class through public employment. During the 1970s, however, economic recession and labor force contraction, abetted by a national policy of urban neglect and ultimately neoliberalization, worked together to produce the hyper-ghettoization of the black poor. In the popular imagination, blackness became a synonym for poor, urban, indebted, uneducated, criminal, imprisoned, and dependent, even though the actual history and demography of the United States since the sixties finds African Americans in the minority for each of these categories, albeit overrepresented.

In that context, the Jim Crow analogy advanced by Michelle Alexander fails to provide an adequate empirical account of the social origins, motives, and consequences of mass incarceration. Alexander emphasizes how the punitive policies of the War on Drugs were intended to, and did, adversely and disproportionately affect blacks.[26] To grasp this development, the Jim Crow analogy has proven to be a powerful and enduring concept for many activists, one that recalls the nation's undemocratic history and undermines popular claims that the country has reached a post-racial epoch where colorblind meritocracy prevails. There are certainly some important parallels between the Jim Crow system and the contemporary prison state, in particular the many ways that convicted felons can be disenfranchised. Even after they have served their prison sentences, ex-offenders can lose the right to vote or participate in jury trials, to receive public assistance and federal student loans, to parental custody and visitation, and to gainful employment due to felon self-reporting requirements on job applications in many states. But the fact remains that the Jim Crow analogy obscures the actual material and social forces that have given rise to the carceral state, specifically the systematic production and reproduction of a surplus population by the contemporary model of capital accumulation that has driven the economy for decades.[27] As the long-term slowdown of investment and GDP growth, beginning in the 1970s, produced increasing numbers of (permanently) unemployed, neoliberals in both parties cut back the welfare state that had initially been established to provide social insurance to the jobless.

Contemporary patterns of incarceration and police violence are classed in a manner that is not restricted to blacks and whose central dynamics cannot be explained through institutional racism. Black professionals can still be subjected to police profiling and abuse; despite their different class position, they remain connected to working-class communities by way of social networks, kinship, and personal origins. These sociological aspects may help to explain the genesis and popularity of the Black Lives Matter hashtag, but they also obscure the essential historical motives of the policing crisis. The urban black poor should not be seen as exceptional, because their ruination is an integral part of the broader political economy. Their plight as a reserve of contingent and unemployed labor is the consequence of neoliberal rollback, technological obsolescence, and informalization, not the revival of Jim Crow racism. The expansion of the carceral state since the seventies has come to replace the welfare state as the chief means of managing social inequality.

Sociologist Loïc Wacquant has used the term "hyperincarceration" rather than "mass incarceration" to more accurately describe what we are witnessing. US incarceration rates dwarf those of other advanced industrial societies, but aggressive policing strategies are not deployed en masse.[28] Rather than a system where all Americans are subject to arrest and incarceration, it is the relative surplus population, often confined to the ghettoized zones of the inner city, blighted inner-ring suburbs, and depopulated Rust Belt towns, who are routinely policed and imprisoned.

The racial justice frame simply does not adequately explain the current crisis of police violence, in which blacks are over-represented but not the majority of victims. In 2015, there were 1,138 people killed by police in the United States, and of that number 581 were white, 306 were black, 195 were Latino, 24 were Asian or Pacific Islander, 13 were Native American, and the race/ethnicity of the remaining 27 was unknown.[29] Rather than prompting some version of "all lives matter" post-racialism, these facts should encourage greater discernment on the part of those who want to create just forms of public safety. The unemployed, the homeless, and those who work in the informal economy or live in areas where that economy is dominant are more likely to be regularly surveilled, harassed, and arrested. Black Lives Matter activists posit universal black injury, where in fact the violence of the carceral state is experienced more broadly across the working class. What is to be gained from adhering to political slogans that exclude certain victims and truncate the potential popular base for progressive reforms?

When confronted with the figure of the white convict, Alexander has argued that he is in fact "collateral damage," the unintended victim in what is a fundamentally anti-black War on Drugs. Even when presented with the contradiction between the Jim Crow analogy and the class dynamics of incarceration, Alexander doubles down and seems to think that referring to nonblack prisoners as collateral damage is still a politically useful approach. "When a white kid in rural Nebraska gets a prison sentence rather than drug treatment he needs but cannot afford, he's suffering because of a drug war declared with Black folks in mind," Alexander contends. "And by describing white people as collateral damage in the drug war it creates an opportunity for us to see the ways in which people of all colors can be harmed by race-based initiatives or attacks that are aimed at another racially defined group."[30] This is a terrible evasion, an attempt to cling to an ideological faith even when actual social conditions require a different approach. The prison expansion and the turn to militaristic hyper-policing are not motivated principally by racism. Whether in Chicago's North Lawndale neighborhood or the Ozark country of southern Missouri, the process of policing the poor is orchestrated by the same diverse cast of beat cops, case managers, probation officers, district attorneys, public defenders, prison guards and wardens, social reformers, conservative and liberal politicians, weapons manufacturers, lobbyists, nonprofits, and foundations: a kind of social control complex that has been growing by leaps and bounds as poverty, cynicism, and the surplus population increase and the neoliberal era grinds on.

Building Popular Consensus, Organizing for Power

The root cause of the contemporary policing and incarceration crisis is not, then, the prevalence of New Jim Crow racism, but rather the advent of zero tolerance policing and prison as the dominant means of managing a huge and growing surplus population in an age where the nation has abandoned the use of state power to guarantee the most basic material needs and protection from market volatility. Of course, reviving the liberal welfare state is itself inadequate to address the current malaise. Contemporary movements must go beyond the limited social amenities extended by mid-twentieth-century capital and create a society where there are no disposable people and where the right to health care, education, housing, and to one's creative capacity and time are not determined and circumscribed by compulsory wage labor.

What should, in any case, be clear is that black ethnic politics is not enough to achieve social justice at this historical juncture. The contemporary struggle against policing has inherited many of the assumptions about black political life and Black Power that took shape during the sixties, even as many activists have criticized the lethargy and conservatism of the black establishment. What we know as black politics is not transhistorical, but the result of Southern desegregation campaigns, Cold War liberal statecraft, and party-patronage machinery, which combined to integrate black politicos and local black constituencies into the New Deal Democratic coalition. Even before the end of Jim Crow segregation, black political life always contained internal ideological diversity and expressed varying class interests. Black political development since the sixties has had the effect of both consolidating an elite-driven politics and identifying the expressed interests of that stratum with those of the black population as a whole.

This belief in common black interest has persisted even as the main material-spatial basis for that mode of thinking, the class-diverse black ghetto of the middle twentieth century, has vanished. As the middle class has gained access to better housing options and as national and local elites advance a new revanchist project of public housing demolition and gentrification, the old racial ghetto has been transformed into a class-exclusive zone. This changing class geography of the black population is reflected in the shifting meaning of the term "ghetto," which has evolved from a sympathetic social designation in the mid twentieth century to an epithet most often used to condemn the alleged cultural pathology of the hyper-segregated and over-policed black poor.

Many on the left have taken a deferential posture toward Black Lives Matter. Some have celebrated this upsurge of activism as the return of black left militancy after decades of movement implosion and stagnancy. Even where they might disagree, many white leftists and some established black figures are clearly uncomfortable airing their ideological and strategic disagreements with millennial black activists for fear of being portrayed as insensitive or unsympathetic.

Those who assert that liberal anti-racism is a necessary phase en route to a more viable working-class left politics either suffer from bad faith or are engaging in the worst form of pandering—namely, supporting black-led political tendencies uncritically as a means of demonstrating one's anti-racist commitments. Those who trade in such patronizing behavior either have not taken the time to study the history of black political life since the sixties or are simply willing to ignore the class contradictions that black communities share with the wider population. Those who cling to liberal anti-racism and defer to essentialist arguments about black interests fail to see that a politics that builds broad solidarity around commonly felt needs and interests *is* a form of anti-racism, one that we desperately need right now if we are to have any chance of ending the policing crisis and creating a more civilized society.

The hegemony of identitarianism has reshaped the terms of left political debate and action in at least three detrimental ways. First, it has engendered popular confusion about political life, leading many to falsely equate social identity with political interests. Second, it has distorted how we understand the work of building alliances not on identity as such, but on shared values and demonstrated commitment. Third, the practice of relying on racial or other identities as a means of authorizing speakers has had a corrupting effect on left political struggles. The result is a degraded public sphere where all manner of land mines prohibit honest discussion and impose limits on political constituency and left imagination, such as notions of "epistemic deference," "mansplaining," arbitrary stipulations about "being an ally," and so forth.

Contemporary battles against police violence and the carceral state address the sharpest edge of late capitalism and represent the struggle of the most submerged segments of the working class to survive under alienated, brutish conditions. Discourses of black difference, whether in the form of Cold War liberal anti-racism, the colonial analogy, or contemporary Black Lives Matter rhetoric, forestall the development of an analysis that would treat the black urban poor not as separate and unique but as a dramatic manifestation of the precarity that defines working-class life more generally.

Black Lives Matter protestors have advanced an inspiring set of demands, but without effective power these will remain in the realm of the imagination. As popular slogans, "Black Power" and "Black Lives Matter" are both significant in opening the door to forms of social struggle that were not relegated strictly to the workplace but addressed to a broader late capitalist geography. To the extent that they remain circumscribed by notions of racial affinity, contemporary campaigns against police violence and the carceral state, like Black Power struggles decades before, will fall short of creating the kind of deep, expansive opposition needed to exact real change. Such struggles must craft broad popular support if they are to succeed where others have failed.

On that December evening when my kids and I joined a dozen or so Chicagoans to watch Samb's performance, I thought back for a moment to the live mannequins who amused the Christmas shoppers of my childhood. Back then, crowds stood fixated on floodlit store displays and wondered aloud how long the performer could remain in character. Samb's performance seemed to pose the question in reverse: Would *we* break from character? His haunting imagery urged us to separate historical process from nostalgia, and political life from consumerism. Without the kind of protracted political engagement and real commitment that stretches beyond cadre and mass demonstrations, we run the risks of reducing social struggle to expressions of consumer niche identity, like the T-shirts, viral memes, and nouveau race films that Black Lives Matter has already spawned. As Samb's provocation reminds us, we can draw inspiration from past heroics, but the solutions we need must be worked out in and for our times. The actual demography of hyper-incarceration and the policing crisis requires that we organize against inherited urban-suburban political divisions, daily habits, clichéd thinking, and familiar social relations to discover common interests and popular power. There can be no end to hyper-incarceration, the policing crisis, and the underlying inequality without the difficult work of taking power and imposing a more democratic and humane order.

2

Black Political Life and the Blue Lives Matter Presidency

Cedric Johnson

My 2017 *Catalyst* article "The Panthers Can't Save Us Now" was addressed to a specific conundrum within contemporary left politics and anti-policing struggles in particular: that is, the strategic problem of building a counterpower capable of winning in the context of renascent black nationalist thinking, sheepishness on the left about class analysis, and a pervasive reluctance to think about black political life with much sophistication.

In a sense, the article was less about the historical Black Panther Party for Self-Defense than the dangers of the sixties nostalgia that afflicts contemporary struggles, namely the revival of racial essentialism, the colonial analogy, and vanguardist posturing. Such notions were limited as a means of advancing black political life during the sixties, and inasmuch as they preserve the fiction that society-wide, revolutionary changes can be won either by the actions of numerical minorities or sectarian tendencies, they are ill-suited to the challenges we face today.

My argument then and now is that Black Lives Matter, and cognate notions such as the New Jim Crow, have been useful in galvanizing popular outrage over policing and mass incarceration, but these same banners have simultaneously enshrouded the very social relations they claim to describe and led away from the kind of politics—one predicated on building broad, popular power—that is necessary to roll back the carceral state. That 2017 article was conceived as a historical materialist antidote to racially reductionist thinking and attempted to excavate the origins of black ethnic politics as we know it.

A key conceptual distinction here is between black ethnic politics—that mode of ethnic representational and electoral practices that was expanded and institutionalized nationally through the confluence of civil rights reform and Black Power mobilizations—and black political life—the heterogeneous, complex totality of shifting positions, competing interests, contradictory actions and behaviors that constitute black political engagement historically. That 2017 article was written as a plea for a more mature view of black political life, and a left politics that proceeded from careful analysis of society as it exists toward building popular constituencies around a more just vision of what society might be.

This essay expands the arguments of my *Catalyst* article by addressing the prevailing hesitation to engage in class analysis of black life. Many left activists and academics continue to abide the notion of black exceptionalism: that there is something unique and incommensurable about the experiences of blacks that prohibits any substantive discussion of class position and interests whenever the black population is concerned. This posture is wrong and dangerous. It is not grounded in any close empirical sense of actually existing black life, but retreats toward the most unidimensional sense of the black population as noble, long-suffering victims of oppression and the moral conscience of a white-dominated nation, rather than as a people possessing all the social contradictions, ideological diversity, foibles, heroism, and frailties found throughout the American populace.

This failure to understand the complexities of black political life leaves intellectuals and activists unable to see the ways that particular segments of the black population, both elites and popular constituencies, have historically supported the carceral expansion and continue to play a crucial role in the reproduction of the highly unequal, unjust neoliberal urban order. Genuflecting before identitarian politics, whether under the guise of Black Power nostalgia or Black Lives Matter sloganeering, does little to help us understand and contest these power alignments. The second part of this essay offers a brief overview of these concomitant processes of black governance, central-city revanchism, and mass incarceration.

This essay concludes by addressing the Trump phenomenon and the clear problems his ascendancy poses, as of early 2019, for anti-policing struggles going forward. Trump is a dangerous figure, and his first term has put his oafishness, sexism, racism, and incivility on full display, but as some have noted, Trump's tweets and antics are a distraction. He is no doubt a powerful booster for authoritarian policing and securitization, but even if he were removed from office before the end of his first term, the carceral state, which has been built up through local- and state-level legislation over the course of decades, would remain; its legitimacy is anchored much deeper within American life and institutions. Moreover, the myth that Trump rode into office on a wave of resurgent white supremacy has only entrenched liberal anti-racist posturing, overgeneralizations about and demonization of white workers, and a prevailing sense that popular left politics are not only out of reach, but not even worth pursuing.

Class and Actually Existing Black Life

The last few years have seen the resurgence of racially reductionist thinking about black political life and a corresponding political defeatism regarding class solidarity. Such thinking is sedimented and reproduced through social media discussions, which are at best proto-political but often anti-political, precluding public-spirited conversation and the possibility of communion and action in face-to-face contexts. Not only has the explosive popularity of social media sites like Facebook and Twitter, as well as the expansion of blogging and podcast platforms, displaced the centrality of corporate news sources in the lives of many Americans, but these media have also produced an artificial leveling in terms of public debate. In this new landscape, access is more universal, but expertise and rigorous investigation are devalued in spaces where sensationalism, conspiracy, and dilettantism breed and flourish underneath ebullient travel photos, cat memes, fish-kiss selfies, and cute toddler videos.

The revival of race-centric approaches to thinking about inequality did not begin with Black Lives Matter. For decades, liberal think tanks, civil rights organizations, and academics working in area studies have promoted various strands of liberal anti-racism. But we might trace the more recent origins of the Black Lives Matter/New Jim Crow frame to the optics of the 2005 Hurricane Katrina disaster and the subsequent ways both academics and activists came to understand the 2008 foreclosure crisis.

Rapper Kanye West may have offered the most memorable statement of this sensibility when he went off-script during a live telethon for Katrina survivors. "America is set up to help the poor, the black people, the less well-off, as slow as possible," West said, before punctuating his impromptu speech with the charge that "George Bush doesn't care about black people." His conviction, that racism was the primary motive for the death and misery in New Orleans, has been rearticulated and expanded in a small library of books and essays over the past decade. *The Nation* columnist Mychal Denzel Smith claims that for his cohort of black millennials, West's words were "our first relatable expression of black rage on a national stage," and that expression has since inspired resurgent waves of black political activity, from the election of Barack Obama to the anti-police brutality protests in Ferguson and Baltimore.[1] Given the media optics of the Katrina crisis, where thousands of black residents crowded the Superdome in search of relief, it is not surprising that so many concluded the disaster was caused by structural racism.

The focus on racial disparity gets much of the Katrina story wrong, however, because it substitutes metanarratives of racial oppression for a more critical and rigorous analysis of the city as a totality, the place-specific institutional and social roots of the disaster, the balance of class forces on the ground, and the power of actual constituencies in shaping disaster preparation and recovery policies in New Orleans—none of which is simply reducible to the legacies of Jim Crow segregation or the hubris of the Bush administration alone. A more critical post-Katrina literature and cinema has situated the governmental failures of disaster evacuation and relief, and the highly uneven politics of reconstruction, within the volatile and crisis-laden processes of urban neoliberalization.[2]

The racial-justice frame does not discern class contradictions within the black population and the variegated experiences of recovery. This framing fails to capture how the contraflow evacuation process worked effectively for middle-class blacks with access to cars, as it had for whites of similar means. The property owner–centered reconstruction programs supported by city, state, and federal governments also helped middle-class homeowners, black and white, to restore their property and lives, while the same governing coalition pushed a wave of evictions and public housing demolitions that created hardship for black working-class residents and made it more difficult for them to return.

In the wake of the "race-class" debates that accompanied the 2016 Democratic presidential primary challenge of democratic socialist and Vermont senator Bernie Sanders, many within academe and activist circles have sought to defend the virtues of identity-based appeals and organizing strategies. The defenses often begin from an interpretation of US history that sees popular, cosmopolitan forms of left alliance as anomalous and too often doomed by the reactionary behaviors and interests of whites, sometimes with the most venom reserved for the "white working class," often portrayed as though it constitutes a self-conscious and unified social category in utero.

Such anti-left populist arguments are often guided by an odd view of history, devoid of any useful sense of conjuncture, and positing wrongly that what did not work in the past clearly will not work now, so why bother. This posture not only sweeps aside meaningful and plentiful examples of cross-racial class solidarity in the US past but also amounts to a loser's view of political life, lacking imagination and courage. The Trump phenomenon, and the prevailing myth that his presidency was the result of resurgent white supremacy and not the reverse, has only further intensified hyperbolic racialist arguments and antipathy toward class analysis and working-class solidarity in some corners.

What the Debate Gets Wrong

Asad Haider's 2018 monograph *Mistaken Identity* is addressed to this new context of Trumpism and attempts to recuperate what he sees as the more radical, progressive origins of identity politics in the nexus of the black political struggles and second-wave feminism of the seventies.[3] Haider reminds us that the phrase "identity politics" was coined by black lesbian feminist activists who formed the Combahee River Collective (CRC), but their initial formulation, which sought to bring anti-racist and anti-sexist sensibilities in as correctives to the limitations of revolutionary socialism as they saw it, was ultimately appropriated and corrupted by liberal elites.

Although he makes numerous references to the CRC's participation in strike actions, and reproductive rights and domestic violence activism, Haider does not pause to evaluate the relative political impact and utility of the CRC vis-à-vis other organizations that actually made life demonstrably better for the greatest number of African Americans. That is to say, we know that the group is significant in the genealogy of black feminism and women's studies as that scholarly discipline evolved out of the sixties and seventies migration of activists into academe, but what political victories can we point to that make CRC an indispensable vein for the contemporary left to mine, especially for strategic lessons concerning building powerful left opposition? Why should we focus on the CRC and not the Congress of Industrial Organizations, the Montgomery Improvement Association, the various grassroots organizations and networks that elected Harold Washington to the Chicago mayoralty in 1983, or for that matter, The Links, Incorporated?

Let us be clear. The CRC emerged during a period of pervasive demobilization, amid the jetsam of Black Power, women's liberation, and the New Left, literally on the eve of the Reagan revolution, and despite whatever interpretative value we might wring from their critique of US society, there is no practical reason to afford the CRC with a privileged place in contemporary left strategic and tactical thinking. Haider is not alone here but rather indulges a common practice of many academics: confusing the scholarly subject that piques one's curiosity, and may be interesting within the novelty-driven dynamics of academic credentialing, conferencing, and publishing, with those historical phenomena that are politically impactful and resonant.

Setting aside this problem of the CRC's historical amplitude and relevance to contemporary efforts to revitalize the left, a bigger problem with Haider's analysis is his neglect of how the empowerment discourse of new social movements emerges from a peculiar deployment of standpoint epistemology, the view descended from Hegel and Marx that those who endure similar social conditions possess common ways of knowing the world. For Marx, the common predicament of the proletariat alone did not generate solidarity; rather, such was clearly the outcome of political organizing and social struggle. Sixties appropriations of standpoint epistemology, however, often falsely equated common predicament, the experience of the black ghetto or of patriarchal order, with shared political sympathy and interests.

Haider is well aware of the ways that identity politics and intersectionality have become corrupted and misused in the time of Black Lives Matter, too often deployed as a means of making territorial-knowledge claims, staking out authority based on relative disadvantage (epistemic deference), and undermining the prospects of open democratic engagement and the possibility of solidarity. We agree on these latter-day problems. Haider sees some value in the prelapsarian version of identity politics first articulated by the CRC, but his historical account forgets how sixties and seventies black radical and feminist politics also abided problematic notions of standpoint epistemology that conflated identity with political constituency.

Standpoint epistemology forms the foundation of identity politics, whether articulated in Stokely Carmichael and Charles Hamilton's 1967 manifesto, *Black Power*, which was heavily informed by the ethnic pluralist claims of Cold War American political science; in the Panthers' desire to liberate the "black colony" within American inner cities, which was in practice ethnic pluralism with anti-colonial patina; in Amiri Baraka's work to forge an institutional mechanism for national black political unity; or even in the CRC's efforts to infuse socialism with analyses of interlocking oppressions. In the classic CRC statement that Haider celebrates, the territoriality he rightly condemns in latter-day movement circles was already gestating: "This focusing on our own oppression is embodied in the concept of identity politics. We believe the most profound and potentially most radical politics came directly out of our own identity, as opposed to working to end somebody else's oppression."[4]

The tendency to equate racial and ethnic identity with political constituency did not first emerge within African American political life during the sixties, but was already hegemonic, a consequence of the exclusion of the black masses from civic life for the first half of the twentieth century, the prevalence of Jim Crow racism beyond the Mason-Dixon line, and the ethnic patron-clientelist practices that dominated most urban governing regimes during the Fordist era. The view of sacrosanct racial constituency, however, is tough to abide when we take a closer look at black political life during the sixties, which was rife with public debate and political rivalry, teeming with different agendas, priorities, and class interests despite the prevailing popular expressions of black unity and soul power.

Haider's critical claim that liberal identity politics is the "neutralization of movements against racial oppression" is an earnest restatement of the familiar co-optation thesis that falls flat when the internal contradictions and limitations of those movements are subjected to rigorous analysis and scrutiny.[5] These black movements were not simply neutralized by the machinations of elites; rather, as many historians and social scientists have illustrated, sixties black political tendencies abided the same flawed logic of racial constituency that Haider sees as emerging at a later point in history.

Black Power was not some grassroots phenomenon that sprung up organically only to be quelled by agents of the state. Black Power took shape within a context of omnibus civil rights reforms; the ongoing evolution and internal debates of interracial organizations, like the Student Nonviolent Coordinating Committee and the Congress of Racial Equality, who helped secure such reforms; the work of sympathetic national politicians and liberal benefactors who sincerely wanted to improve the lives of black Americans, albeit under the terms of the postwar consumer society; the Johnson administration's War on Poverty, which provided federal block grants to develop anti-poverty programs at the local level; and the growing sense in black neighborhoods and communities nationwide that shifting demographic and political conditions made increased black control of governing institutions a real possibility. What the calls for black power and self-determination came to mean in operational terms cannot be separated out from the broader urban and national political processes that shaped black life during the last days of Jim Crow segregation. There is more to African American political development than the heroic political tendencies that leftists fetishize.

Against left critics of identity politics, Haider claims that there is a "materiality of race" as a social relation.[6] This is the formulation du jour for some on the left, but when applied to black social life beyond the originary context of antebellum slavery, it is a conceptual evasion that evokes material conditions only to make a racially reductionist point about some common predicament of blacks (or whites) regardless of class position. If the notion were to have any integrity as an analytic frame, then Haider and others would need to actually explore in greater depth the historically specific material conditions, the situated class experiences of blacks under capitalism.

Such analyses would include not only the sharecroppers union, the Scottsboro Boys' legal defense campaign, or the League of Revolutionary Black Workers—favorite topics of the academic left that Haider evokes in a Verso blog defense of his book.[7] Any helpful discussion of the "materiality of race" would also need to take seriously those manifestations of bourgeois class position, aspiration, and ideology that contend for influence within black political life at every historical juncture and often secure legitimacy and devotion among layers of the black working class—for instance the reign of Tuskegee Machine; the role of the Afro-American Realty Company in the making of Harlem; the Geddes Willis Funeral Home and scores of others in every major city and small town with a sizable black population; the business ventures of black entrepreneurs such as Jesse Binga, Madame C.J. Walker, A.G. Gaston, and legions of other race women and men; the black professional organizations that were also born out of Black Power; the anti–public housing stances of black New Democrats; the expansion of black tourist-entertainment niches such as the annual Essence Fest; and on and on.

"A materialist mode of investigation," Haider contends, "has to go from the abstract to the concrete—it has to bring this abstraction back to earth by moving through all the historical specificities and material relations that have put it in our heads."[8] This particular outing for Haider, however, falls short of making good on that methodological commitment.

Throughout the text, Haider offers pithy statements about the centrality of race and anti-racism to revitalizing the left. "As long as racial solidarity among whites is more powerful than class solidarity across races," he writes, "both capitalism and whiteness will continue to exist." "In the context of American history," Haider continues, "the rhetoric of the 'white working class' and positivist arguments that class matters more than race reinforce one of the main obstacles to building socialism."[9]

Of course, it is quite possible for capitalism to exist without white racial domination in the United States, as it does in other parts of the world—think Lagos. Also, we have already witnessed in many American cities how heritage tourism, ethnic cultural markers (such as Mexican murals, blues music trails, immigrant commercial thoroughfares, etc.), and multiracial coalitions have been central to place branding, real estate valuation, and neighborhood revitalization in ways that facilitate capital accumulation and the empowerment of some people of color alongside the massive displacement of others. As well, despite Haider's historicist point about the "main obstacles to building socialism," there are powerful examples of biracial and interracial unionism, where anti-black racism among workers was clearly an impediment to organizing but ultimately did not prevent striking dockworkers and teamsters in postbellum New Orleans, or miners in the West Virginia Coal Wars, from achieving meaningful solidarity and collective advance.

Such ambitious statements may score points in the seminar room or basement study group, but this rhetoric, however well intentioned, has little to do with the internal workings of political life, how people perceive their immediate interests and priorities in real time and space—union drives, city council campaigns, class action lawsuits against polluters, parent-teacher meetings about pending state tests, and the like—contexts where race and class are not always the chief preoccupations or animating logics among citizens that left activists and academics suppose them to be.

The underlying claim in *Mistaken Identity*—that foregrounding anti-racism might secure more extensive commitments of people of color to the nominal left—is shopworn, unproven, and descended from the recruitment strategies of the Socialist Workers Party during the sixties and still prevalent among elements of the International Socialist Organization and the revived Democratic Socialists of America. This strategic posture, which reduces the expressed needs and diverse interests of blacks, Latinx, and other people of color to the "struggle against racial oppression," is at best misguided, at worst patronizing, and will continue to lead us toward a dead end.

To his credit, Haider does allude to the sharpening of class conflict within post-segregation black political life, especially in a chapter dedicated to the life and serial ideological conversions of the late poet and activist Amiri Baraka. This discussion of class and black politics, however, is rather perfunctory, derivative, and at a level of theoretical abstraction that dances above the moil of black political life as it is experienced in everyday social relations, grounded organizational contexts, and historical class interests in motion. It would seem that a focus on these quotidian matters would be central in a book that hopes to rescue some radical kernel of sixties and seventies identity politics from latter-day appropriations and use whatever lessons gained to build left opposition in the present.

I am not suggesting that Haider needed to address the full spectrum of black political tendencies and personalities in this particular book, which is clearly intended as a provocation and work of theory rather than accurate interpretation grounded in a deep reading of historiography and primary sources. It would seem, however, that the most useful normative political theory, especially one that evokes Lenin's "concrete analysis of concrete conditions," would be informed by a more critical-empirical understanding of black life as it exists, especially when twentieth-century black political developments and the "black radical tradition," which is essentially an exercise in canon formation, are used to underwrite his claims.

Put another way, if black political life has become more complicated over the last half century by the extensive integration of the black population into the consumer society, the expansion of the black middle class, the process of black political incorporation, and the worsening conditions of the most submerged segments of the black working class, why should we recuperate racial identity politics, however refined, as a framework for understanding our times and as a basis for political organizing?

In line with Haider, political scientist Joe Lowndes casts doubt on left analyses that criticize the limits of racial identity politics in favor of class solidarity. In a 2018 *Baffler* essay assessing the perils of left- and right-wing populism, Lowndes laments, "Populism is as populism does," before concluding that "just as right-wing populism draws on democratic and egalitarian desires, left-wing variants can have a cramped notion of the people that alienates the politically vulnerable and marginal."[10] To illustrate the historical problems of populism, Lowndes rehearses an all-too-familiar "constraint of race" narrative, an interpretation of American political development where socialist and progressive left politics are undermined as white workers are time and again seduced by the siren song of reactionary politics, siding with the power of capital and against people of color, from Jacksonianism through the rise of the New Right.

It is difficult to dispute the broad outlines of this account. The United States is a nation founded on African chattel slavery, indentured servitude, the conquest and removal of indigenous peoples, the disenfranchisement of the unpropertied, and the domestication and exclusion of women from full civic life—a condition that would last for over half of the nation's history. The devil does not live in the granular details of history but rather sets up his workshop in the generalities and occlusions of such "constraint of race" narratives. As with Haider's *Mistaken Identity*, the level of abstraction in Lowndes's account actually leads away from the kind of critical historical analysis that might reveal the rich and contradictory archive of working-class struggles, the specific conjunctural challenges we face now, and those quotidian concerns that may form the basis for building viable left opposition.

As is common nowadays, Lowndes offers the obligatory criticism of the New Deal. Franklin D. Roosevelt's "vision shored up producerist ideology," Lowndes writes, "a strictly gendered division of labor, and, through the distinction between 'entitlements' and 'relief,' a sharp divide between the deserving and undeserving poor." This is certainly true, but there is more to the story. The New Deal coalition under Roosevelt's leadership shored up a consumerist ideology as well. Indeed, he saw raising the vast consumer capacity of Americans as a remedy for the problems of overproduction that in part precipitated the Great Depression. Likewise, as a consequence of labor shortages and mass activist pressure during World War II, Roosevelt's administration was compelled to momentarily break down racial and gendered divisions of labor through integration of the defense industries. This historical development is significant and prefigures the postwar civil rights movement and the birth of second-wave feminism, but such facts get in the way of the kind of criticism of left populism Lowndes wants to craft.

We should be fully aware of the patent limitations of midcentury American liberalism and the inequalities produced by the New Deal coalition, especially the real estate–driven growth trajectory established after World War II. But Lowndes's accounting, like so many others, leaves out the ways that the expansion of the social wage and labor protections, and the institution of national public works initiatives like the Works Progress Administration and the Civilian Conservation Corps, benefited African Americans in unprecedented ways. Lowndes's summary thesis, which repeats claims that have become conventional wisdom in some corners of the left, does damage to the complex legacy of the New Deal and underwrites a left cynicism we cannot afford.

Oddly enough, Lowndes's account of the misadventures of populism does not mention the pervasive power of Cold War red-baiting and witch hunts against Communists and leftist trade unionists. This domestic trench warfare against the left played out in the televised hearings of the House Un-American Activities Committee, FBI interrogation rooms, police raids, death threats, imprison-ment, the financial ruin of accused reds, and disappearances and assassinations, and it would have a lasting impact on the American left, dividing the laboring classes against them-selves and defeating more progressive-to-radical left political possibilities. It would seem that this grim episode would be central to any intellectual appreciation of the difficulty of building a viable left populism.

Lowndes insists, "We need a left-wing populism that puts anti-racism, immigrant rights, and refugee solidarity at the center of its politics." If Lowndes's point here is simply that progressive left and socialist organizations must confront reactionary thinking and behaviors—anti-black racism, xenophobia, Islamophobia, anti-Semitism, misogyny, homo-phobia, and so on—whenever they arise in the actual context of organizing and building solidarity, then there is little here that anyone with progressive left or socialist commitments should find disagreeable. In the particular context of policing and prison reforms, activists must, for instance, contest and overturn hegemonic underclass narratives that treat poverty as a consequence of the alleged cultural failings and behav-iors of the poor and that justify mass incarceration and puni-tive social policy. The problem with such declarations that we centralize anti-racism, however, is that in many local political battles and campaigns, race and racism are not always a central concern.

Moreover, the liberal anti-racist frame reduces what are in fact common class conditions felt more widely across racial and ethnic populations to matters of racism and racial disparity. To emphasize the need to centralize anti-racism, Lowndes closes out by praising the militant protests that erupted in the Bay Area following the killing of Oscar Grant by transit police, the battles against ICE deportations, and other struggles he sees as "opening out onto broader vistas with populist dimensions." Those vistas could be broader still, especially when we take seriously the actual patterns of police abuse, which defy liberal anti-racist canards.

Of the ten cities with the highest per capita fatal police shootings of civilians, only one approaches a majority-black population—Baton Rouge (50.4 percent black), followed closely by St. Louis (49.2 percent) with Las Vegas trailing well behind (11.1 percent). Of the remaining cities, the black population constituted less than 3 percent: Kingman, Arizona (0.04 percent black); Las Cruces, New Mexico (2.4 percent); Billings, Montana (0.08 percent); Pueblo, Colorado (2.4 percent); Rapid City, South Dakota (1.1 percent); Westminster, Colorado (1.2 percent); and Casper, Wyoming (1 percent). Black Lives Matter protests have galvanized opposition to police abuse, but clearly there are neighborhoods and communities in the US hinterlands that some on the left have written off, that endure over-policing, violence, and precarity but fall out of the race-centric, metropolitan framing of these problems favored by activists and academics.

Evocations of the "materiality of race," or "confronting the meanings of race," especially as prerequisites for building a majoritarian left politics, are a ruse. These are more sophisticated statements of Black Lives Matter sloganeering; they are valuable as a means of signaling one's ethico-political commitments in academe and within majority-white left sectarian circles and social media networks.

Race is not always the central axis of conflict, nor the primary organizing impediment in local contexts, in the dominant sense that Haider or Lowndes might have us believe—not even among black people. We should certainly condemn and fight racism in all its manifestations. However, in political life, we should also proceed from a careful investigation of the felt needs, shifting political positions, and expressed interests of blacks and all other Americans, rather than assuming black exceptionalism—that African Americans constitute a discrete political constituency who can never find common cause with nonblacks. This is simply not true. The irrationality and falsehood of such thinking becomes especially clear when we rehearse the historical evolution of the carceral state, which was made possible through a circuitous and tragic combination of a social forces that were not limited to the Reagan-Bush rendition of the War on Drugs, white suburban voter anxieties, and myths of black criminality alone.

The path toward building the popular opposition that is needed to produce substantial criminal justice reforms does not begin with "confronting the meanings of race" as a therapeutic or proselytory stance, but rather with a clear sense of the peculiar political alliances that have produced our current order and the difficult work of changing public perceptions and securing support for more just forms of public safety.

Policing the Revanchist City

The expansion of the carceral state and more aggressive policing of urban minority communities coincided with the rollback of the welfare state at the national level, and the almost-
universal pursuit of urban downtown redevelopment as an
antidote to the loss of manufacturing jobs in many US cities.

As others have noted, the carceral buildup of the late War on
Drugs era was not merely the handiwork of conservative
Republicans. Rather, mass incarceration was the creation of
various constituencies—black and white; urban, suburban, and
rural; liberal and conservative; New Democrats, black nationalists, victims' families, drug rehabilitation clinicians, social workers, and community activists—who supported expanded police
protection, more punitive sentencing laws, increased funding
for prisons, and the like. Some supported these policies for
staunchly ideological reasons, while others did so out of desper-
ation, seeing punishment as the only plausible cure for worsening crime and social disorder, especially as the tangible benefits
of social democracy were no longer part of the lived experiences
and popular memory of millions of Americans.

The roots of this dilemma lie in the Cold War liberal turn
away from public works and redistributive public policy and
toward civil society and cultural solutions to urban poverty.
Moreover, the ramping up of the War on Drugs during the
Reagan-Bush years coincided with an intensifying class war
and the aggressive removal of the poor from the urban center,
where the policing strategy of pacification was central to the
postindustrial growth model driven by the financial, insurance,

and real estate industry and the tourism-entertainment sector. The late geographer Neil Smith characterized this process in terms of the "revanchist city."[11]

While the postwar transformation of the urban landscape created physical distance between the new suburban middle class and those left ghettoized in the inner-city core, the taking back of the city through gentrification and real estate valorization beginning in the eighties brought these disparate classes into direct confrontation—with middle-class urban pioneers, the investor class, and tourists on one side, and minority communities, the unemployed, the itinerant poor, and countercultural enclaves on the other. "This revanchist anti-urbanism," Smith holds,

> represents a reaction against the supposed "theft" of the city, a desperate defense of a challenged phalanx of privileges, cloaked in the populist language of civic morality, family values, and neighborhood security.
>
> . . . More than anything the revanchist city expresses a race/class/gender terror felt by middle- and ruling-class whites who are suddenly stuck in place by a ravaged property market, the threat and reality of unemployment, the decimation of social services, and the emergence of minority and immigrant groups, as well as women, as powerful urban actors.

Smith continues, "It portends a vicious reaction against minorities, the working class, homeless people, the unemployed, women, gays and lesbians, immigrants."[12]

These processes of revanchism have occurred in fits and starts, more successful in some cities than others, but securitization has been at the heart of this phenomenon, making the city safe for more upwardly mobile residents and visitors. Pacification and removal of the poor, architectural innovation, and new forms of enclosure have produced a new central-city landscape—one where class contradictions are managed through manifold technologies of policing, surveillance, and certification that permit ease of movement across urban space for those of economic means while regulating and constricting the poor. This is a new metropolitan landscape defined by Airbnb, Uber, helipads for the nouveau riche, artisanal grocers, novelty fitness clubs, private roads, and relentless condo tower construction, and equally by bum-proof benches and ankle monitors, pretext police stops, the demolition of public housing, ubiquitous closed-circuit cameras, a criminalized and informal economy, predatory lenders, and check-cashing centers.

One immediate casualty of this new urban warfare, as historian and urbanist Mike Davis reported some time ago, was the elimination of the very notion of the public. "The universal consequence of the crusade to secure the city is the destruction of any truly democratic urban space," Davis wrote. "The American city is being systematically turned inward. The 'public' spaces of the new megastructures and supermalls have supplanted traditional streets and disciplined spontaneity."[13] This war on the public has created new opportunities for profit-making and philanthropy for the investor class, and made already-vulnerable segments of the working class even more desperate, insuring a ready and cheap reservoir of servant labor. These processes of urban fortressing were further entrenched in the wake of the 9/11 terrorist attacks, which precipitated a wave of federal and state spending on policing and surveillance programs under the pretext of national security.

At the center of these processes of urban neoliberalization and revanchism was the liberal black political elite who governed many American cities through a period of manufacturing decline and postindustrial renaissance. Their complex role is neglected in most accounts of the carceral buildup, yet the fact of multiracial support for policing and incarceration remains a formidable barrier to the kinds of reforms promoted through Black Lives Matter protests.

In the decades after demands for black power, black political incorporation became a reality, with most major American cities electing black mayors and often majority-black city councils. These black-led cities, however, would inherit a number of well-known constraints on their capacity to govern, such as declining tax bases, population loss, capital flight, the drought in federal investment, the expanded power of bond-rating agencies and international financiers, antiquated infrastructure, and deteriorating social conditions. Likewise, the class-diverse black ghettoes of the mid twentieth century, which provided the spatial-demographic basis for Black Power demands for indigenous control, would undergo dramatic transformation, producing the hypersegregation of the black poor. Within this dire context, citizens and civic leaders made even more difficult policy choices, with some blacks supporting anti-crime measures because of idiosyncratic political beliefs and others because of their specific constituent interests as homeowners, shopkeepers, or victims' families.

Some common maneuvers, whenever the subject of black class politics is broached, are to emphasize the relative precariousness of the black professional-managerial class when compared to whites or to downplay the relative power of black political elites in public affairs. The first move is usually intended to shore up the view that race remains the primary social determinant in American life, which is not a difficult argument to make given the many documented disparities in wealth and income, even between blacks and whites of similar levels of educational attainment. The second move is pitched for much the same reasons, to emphasize that even blacks who occupy positions of institutional authority will likely be constrained by the power of reactionary, superordinate whites—a claim that seems infallible during the reign of the New Right and the New Democrats.

Class is not fundamentally a matter of gradations of income, but rather a matter of relative power within the social relations of production. The black middling and elite classes have certainly been historically smaller and generally more vulnerable than similarly situated whites. Despite its relative size and precarity, however, the black professional-managerial class often plays a role in society, especially during the post-segregation era, that many whites cannot fulfill: the role of legitimating and advancing Democratic Party politics and neoliberal privatization agendas at the local level. This is a social role that whites cannot play effectively given prevailing notions of black racial constituency, cementing black public consent and mediating the demands of popular and working-class constituencies, whose interests are often at odds with the dictates of city hall and the Washington Beltway. That said, conservative, pro-policing attitudes and interests are not strictly limited to African American elites; at various moments, specific local black constituencies have embraced tough-on-crime measures, especially during the epoch of neoliberalization, when the expansion of progressive social spending became increasingly difficult to pursue.

Yale law professor James Forman Jr. offers a highly textured account of how and why some residents, politicians, and activists in Washington, DC, supported a politics of incarceration during an era of black political control.[14] In his study, we find historically discrete motives for black support of various anti-crime and pro-policing policies. Black civil rights activists in Atlanta during the forties and in the District of Columbia in the sixties demanded the hiring of more black officers as a remedy to police brutality. During the seventies, black nationalists opposed marijuana legalization in the district because they viewed it as a "gateway" drug to more debilitating addictions. Some black judges insisted on harsh punishment for black violent offenders out of a moral obligation to black victims, who for too long were denied adequate police protection or court justice under Jim Crow. These decisions were made with an eye toward what might be done to reduce addiction, theft, and violence in black communities within a context of limited choices.

The stories Forman presents contradict contemporary anti-racist sloganeering and analyses that portray the problems of policing and mass incarceration in stark black-and-white terms. Instead, he gives a more nuanced historical account of why certain urban black constituencies supported policies that would eventually have disastrous effects on black incarceration rates. He also illustrates, through a close analysis of attitudes toward policing in black professional and working-class neighborhoods, that there are distinct class experiences of policing, with working-class blacks more likely to be subjected to intensive and routine police surveillance and arrests.

Forman's work presents us with a political paradox that remains instructive in this era of resurgent liberal identity politics—that is, the fact of black political control did not protect black district residents from the escalating problems of crime and policing. Rather, within the all-black context of the district, different constituencies combined to produce measures, like mandatory minimum sentencing laws, that had unintended consequences, contributing to the problem of mass incarceration. Racial affinity and ascriptive status should not be mistaken for political constituency, and an understanding of the discrete interests constituting black life will be crucial to any success that police-reform forces hope to achieve going forward. Former New Democratic black mayors like Adrian Fenty in Washington, DC; C. Ray Nagin in New Orleans; and Stephanie Rawlings-Blake in Baltimore presided over a period of urban revanchism where the interests of capital were prioritized over the education, security, and livelihoods of black working-class neighborhoods, and, alongside black contractors and school-privatization advocates, such black leadership has played a crucial role in legitimating neoliberalization by providing it with a multiracial countenance.

In cities like Baltimore and Chicago, which possess integrated police forces and city administrations, massive anti-policing protests have been defused and placated through legal prosecution of police, suspensions, and token firings. Street demonstrations against police abuse have also been met with the mobilization of more centrist black political elements, who have called for modest technical reforms to correct police abuse, such as standard-issue body cameras, and who have advanced private charitable projects and volunteer mentoring as solutions to poverty. Moreover, electoral pressures and activist demands have produced a generation of public relations–savvy black police chiefs, such as Charles Ramsey, former commissioner of the Philadelphia Police Department and before that, head of the District of Columbia's Metropolitan Police Department, and Chicago Police superintendent Eddie Johnson, who have perfected skilled messaging and crisis management.

This is not to say that black top cops do not endorse the same pretext stops, profiling, and aggressive tactics as their white counterparts. Ramsey presided over the mass arrest of protestors and preemptive raids of activist staging areas during the 2000 demonstrations against the World Bank in Washington, DC. Unlike whites, however, they are able to emote effectively with some black audiences, marshal authenticity claims to gain trust from some of the most heavily policed neighborhoods, and deflect charges of racism.

In large and complex urban areas, where black power has long been institutionalized and entrenched, analyses that ignore the actually existing class relations and interests shaping incarceration and the political arena will do little to advance the kind of substantive reforms touted by the most progressive elements of anti-policing protests. The combination of these local challenges produced by multiracial, neoliberal governing coalitions, and the ascension of Donald Trump to the presidency, should encourage activists now more than ever to work toward building broad popular consent for concrete alternatives to the current accumulation regime and its attendant modes of policing.

The Blue Lives Matter Presidency

Securitization and policing, racist exclusion, and repression were central features of Trump's ascension to the presidency. During the summer of 2016, when his election still seemed like a long shot to many, Trump was emphatic in his support for police. He seized upon two separate incidents where police were assaulted by black gunmen, saying, "We must stand in solidarity with law enforcement, which we must remember is the force between civilization and total chaos," echoing the core logic of the "thin blue line" that has animated US law enforcement since the Cold War. Trump led a chorus of conservative voices who claimed that the Obama administration and Black Lives Matter protests had created dangerous conditions for police officers. Former New York City mayor (and later Trump's attorney) Rudolph Giuliani was quick to attack activists, claiming that Black Lives Matter is "inherently racist because, number one, it divides us."

Contrary to the overheated rhetoric of Trump, Giuliani, and others, policing is not the most hazardous occupation in the United States. In fact, it is not even in the top ten, with on-the-job police fatalities ranking well behind those of construction workers, groundskeepers, fishermen and women, garbage collectors, and loggers, among others. And contrary to the claim that the Obama administration enabled anti-police sentiment, violence against police officers actually decreased during Obama's tenure, especially when compared to the George W. Bush years. Moreover, conservative attacks on Black Lives Matter are simply unfounded. White men were responsible for 70 percent of the violence against law enforcement that occurred during the 2016 election year. The mass shootings of police during the 2016 July Fourth week were troubling, but equally so is the fact of police suicide, which in recent years dwarfs the numbers of police officer fatalities by shootings and traffic accidents combined. Yet this concern is not at the forefront of the "Blue Lives Matter" chest thumping of Trump, Giuliani, and their ilk.

Since taking office, Trump has continued to deride any dissent against police violence and abuse. He infamously demanded that the National Football League's team owners fire any player who joined San Francisco 49ers quarterback Colin Kaepernick's national anthem protests. Trump also openly joked about police violence during a 2017 address to law enforcement at Suffolk County Community College in Long Island. He went so far as to encourage rough treatment of suspects during arrests and minimized their right to due process.

Following the weathered playbook of GOP strategists, Trump's approach to campaigning and governing pits the deserving American middle class against the relative surplus population of welfare dependents, the unemployed and unemployables, undocumented migrant workers, and low-wage workers in China and other countries. Surplus population, or the industrial reserve army, is understood here as those persons not currently employed who might be pressed into service to the advantage of capital. Relative surplus population in any given historical context exerts downward pressure on wages. As a reservoir of low-wage, fragmented, and disempowered labor, they are employed as competitors to the relatively more secure segments of the workforce and as such can be used to foment division within the working class.

Since the dismantling of the social wage and the rise of the New Right, the surplus population in the United States has been routinely evoked in campaign rhetoric that places the blame for the general social morass and public finance woes on the continued costs of welfare assistance programs, public support for noncitizens, Medicaid, anti-discrimination regulation in college admissions and private sector hiring, funding for public education, and the pensions of public sector employees. These underserving segments, we are told in every election cycle, do not pay their fair share of taxes and do not contribute much to the economic and social health of the nation.

Blaming the most vulnerable among the working class, however, merely absolves corporate elites of their culpability in producing wage stagnancy and worsening living conditions through their decisions—such as union busting, offshoring, the replacement of living labor with automation, and massive reductions in the taxation of the investor class. Blame-labeling the black urban poor and immigrants further distracts an already-anxious middle class and secures their interests as consumer-citizens to the reproduction of the capitalist order.

Trumpism appeals to the real economic anxieties of those Americans who can recall the last days of a vibrant manufacturing-based economy. His protectionist ideas as well as his xenophobia beckon many Americans, not just whites, back to a nostalgic ideal of unending compound growth and middle-class consumption. This is where the legitimacy of the current carceral order resides, and it is unlikely that progressive left forces can create a more just alternative without engaging broad swaths of the population, wrestling with real and imagined anxieties, fears, and felt needs. Indeed, that is the only way to turn the tide against Trump's authoritarian populism and produce a more just, egalitarian society.

3

Only a Class Politics Can Save Us from Police Violence and Fascism: Lessons from Rosa Luxemburg and Cedric Johnson

Jay Arena

The winter 2019 edition of *New Politics* marks the one-hundredth anniversary of the Social Democratic–led German government's assassination of the towering Polish-born German Marxist revolutionary Rosa Luxemburg, along with her comrade Karl Liebknecht. An appropriate way to commemorate her life and work is the symposium in this issue dedicated to engaging the award-winning essay by political scientist Cedric Johnson "The Panthers Can't Save Us Now." Johnson's class dissection of a black version of ethnic politics, his emphasis on democratic organization and debate for social movement success, his views of the centrality of class struggle at the workplace and in the community, and of the need for unifying class demands all highlight central themes in Luxemburg's work. Below I discuss how Johnson's critique of the Black Lives Matter (BLM) movement elaborates on these Luxemburgist themes and provides a path to addressing not only police killings, but also the larger capitalist assault that drives them.

The Nationalist Line Is a Class Line

A defining feature of Luxemburg's work is a withering critique of all forms of nationalism and what we would now call identity politics. This comes through in her 1896 article "The Polish Question at the International Congress in London," which polemicized against the Fourth Congress of the Second International supporting independence for Poland, to her 1918 work "The Russian Revolution," which critiques Lenin's advocacy of the "right of self-determination of peoples" and was written months before her brutal murder. Luxemburg, in these and other works, always emphasized the bourgeois class interests that lie behind nationalist politics' pretenses of speaking for the whole people.[1] "The famous 'right of self-determination of nations,'" she caustically remarked in her polemic against Lenin's famous thesis, "is nothing but hollow, petty bourgeois phraseology and humbug. Under the rule of capitalism there is no self-determination of peoples . . . In class society each class of the nation strives to 'determine itself' in a different fashion . . . For the bourgeois classes, the standpoint of national freedom is fully subordinated to that of class rule."[2]

Like Luxemburg in critiquing the nationalists—of both the oppressed and oppressor variety—Johnson interrogates the claims of Black Power advocates, such as Stokely Carmichael, co-author of the 1967 classic *Black Power: The Politics of*

Liberation, and the contemporary "Black Power nostalgia" exponents, such as Alicia Garza, co-founder of BLM. They all promote what he terms a problematic "black unity" politics. This politics is rooted in the theory of "black exceptionalism," whose proponents "insist on the uniqueness of the black predicament and on the need for race-specific remedies."[3] According to Garza, a leading light among the new cohort of black unity exponents, blacks of all classes face a world where they "are systematically and intentionally targeted for demise."[4] The political practice that flows from this theory of black oppression is a unified black politics—with white and other "allies" possibly assisting— directed toward combating a set of common oppressions and winning a set of demands that address the needs of a unitary black subject.

Johnson subjects "black unity" political theory and practice to historical interrogation and finds that it has produced what he terms an "elite brokerage politics." This is one that has delivered real material benefits to more privileged layers of African Americans—who invariably speak for and define the interests of the "black community"—while failing to build a mass, democratically based "counterpower" that could deliver real benefits to the black working-class majority. This is clearly seen in the evolution of 1960s Black Power to a 1970s-and-onward black ethnic politics that informs black municipal governance—"really existing Black Power." The fruit of this politics, Johnson finds, has been the "ascendancy of post-segregation patron-client relations between an expanding black professional-managerial class and the mainstream parties, corporations, and private foundations."[5]

BLM activists have attempted to resurrect the rhetoric and trappings of an earlier, radical Black Power version of this politics, with an intersectional twist that now incorporates women and LGBT African Americans. But, as exemplified by leading BLM avatars such as DeRay Mckesson and the three founders of Black Lives Matter—Garza, Patrisse Cullors, and Opal Tometi—these activists replicate the racial broker role. Just as with their older, male, heterosexual competitors whom they seek to displace, they use their mass and social media–conferred movement leadership as "a vehicle," as Johnson argues, "for entrepreneurial branding and courting philanthropic foundations."

Johnson does acknowledge that the black unity politics that informs BLM has produced demands, such as those outlined in the *Vision for Black Lives*, that speak to the needs of black working-class communities. But the class-vacuous language deployed by black unity politics, the "black exceptionalism" theoretical framework from which these activists operate, and their own class origins or aspirations tend to result in "movement" demands being repositioned to address the interests of the affluent and pose no real challenge to the capitalist conditions that produce police killings and terror. The rapid response by Ford and other foundations to the BLM phenomenon, in the form of the $100 million Black-Led Movement Fund—which was embraced by BLM activists, many of whom come out of the nonprofit industrial complex—is designed to guarantee that trajectory.[6]

Like Luxemburg, Johnson unearths the material conditions that guarantee, even more so than in the 1960s and '70s, that a black unity politics will be one that serves the black professional-managerial class and their corporate partners. The enormous expansion in class inequality over the last forty years among African Americans, which is even more pronounced than the gargantuan growth of inequality within the class structure as a whole, makes the search for black unity a chimera.[7] One expression of this growing class divide has been the prominence among the BLMers of charter school supporters and administrators tied to the finance capital that has pushed for privatizing public education and has sold privatization as "the civil rights movement of our day." Yet, due to black unity politics, leaders such as Cullors support working with the increasingly influential black charter school supporters and other black neoliberals.

How Do We End Capitalist Violence?

While critical of BLM and the racial unity politics that informs activists who operate under this umbrella, Johnson does recognize the kernel of "good sense" embodied in the *Vision for Black Lives* agenda. The demands address the oppression and exploitation that black working-class people face at both the workplace and in social reproduction. The importance of a working-class movement addressing the needs of workers on various fronts echoes the criticisms that Luxemburg made in her classic work *The Mass Strike, the Political Party, and the Trade Unions*. In this seminal study, written in 1906, she criticized the social democratic trade union leaders who encouraged workers to "place the highest value on the smallest economic achievement" at the work-place, but who in the process "gradually lose the power of seeing the larger connections and taking a survey of the whole position [of workers]." Thus, while the German trade union leaders at the dawn of the twentieth century congratulated themselves on winning wage gains and shortened hours, they were blind to "the simultaneous and immense reduction of the proletarian standard of life" by such methods as "land usury, by the whole tax and customs policy, by landlord rapacity which has increased house rents to such an exorbitant extent, in short by all the objective tendencies of bourgeois policy which have largely neutralized the advantages of the fifteen years of trade-union struggle."[8]

Luxemburg's emphasis on the whole worker and the need to fight on various fronts, including housing, is central to the political project Johnson advocates. The policing crisis, he emphasizes, cannot be understood as a product of an unchanging, ahistorical "anti-blackness" or a "New Jim Crow." Rather, it must be placed within the larger context of the four-decade capitalist war from above that has led to the marginalization of increasingly wide swaths of the population. The most marginalized have been the primary victims of the police killings, and while they have been disproportionally black, many whites, along with Latinos, Asians, and Native Americans, have been targeted as well. In fact, Johnson emphasizes, contrary to the "New Jim Crow" analogy BLM and other activists use to characterize police killings, whites constitute the largest number of those killed by the police. This underscores for Johnson that only a broad, multiracial class movement can end police violence. This movement must bring in not only the most marginalized, who are so often the targets of police violence, but the broader working class who are also under attack on various fronts, from loss of pensions to outsourcing, home foreclosures, and other forms of capitalist-induced insecurity and dispossession.

To build this movement, one that can draw in large swaths of the working class, Johnson advocates a program that goes well beyond the limited US welfare state. He calls for the decommodification of housing, health care, education, and other basic needs and the creation of well-paying, socially productive, democratically run jobs and workplaces. This would require a mass direct-government program of employment in public works and public services, one on an even a larger scale than what Bayard Rustin and A. Phillip Randolph called for in their *Freedom Budget* of the mid-1960s.

Rustin, like Johnson, "insisted that black progress could only be achieved through the development of broad, interracial coalitions dedicated to social democracy, a position that drew the ire of some Black Power radicals."[9] Presciently, Rustin predicted that the Black Power advocates he crossed swords with in the mid-1960s turning point of the civil rights movement would end up creating a *"new black establishment."*[10] But at the same time, Rustin's strategy of operating within what he called the "consensus party"—the Democrats—including acquiescence to and support for the Vietnam War and the larger US war machine, doomed any chance of winning his much-needed *Freedom Budget*, or even concessions. Johnson's support for Rustin's interracial class politics, while criticizing his later turn to "insider politics," implies that the movement Johnson proposes will need to have its own working-class, democratically controlled political vehicle if it is to make any advances.

Capitalist Barbarism or Revolutionary Socialism

I am finishing this article in the days after the October 28, 2018, election of the fascist Jair Bolsonaro as president of Brazil. Far from an outlier, he is the most dangerous version of a whole layer of fascists, proto-fascists, and authoritarians who have arisen in the decade following the 2008 global capitalist crisis—which continues for broad swaths of the global working class. As Luxemburg powerfully wrote amid the carnage of World War I, either humanity advances toward socialism or we face the further "regression of bourgeois society into barbarism."[11] These words have particular resonance today. Either we provide a real, working-class, socialist solution to the multiple capitalist-produced crises confronting wide swaths of the globe, or the fascists will impose theirs.

To find a path out of the horrors of capitalism requires the global working-class movement to engage in serious criticism of our past mistakes. "Gigantic as his problems are his mistakes," wrote Luxemburg as she sat in a German jail cell in 1915 for her opposition to the war that her former comrades in the German Social Democratic Party supported.

> No firmly fixed plan, no orthodox ritual that holds good for all times, shows him the path he must travel. Historical

experience is his only teacher, his *Via Dolorosa* to freedom is covered not only with unspeakable suffering, but with countless mistakes. The goal of his journey, his final liberation, depends entirely upon the proletariat, on whether *it* understands to learn from *its* own mistakes. *Self-criticism, cruel, unsparing criticism, that goes to the very root of the evil is life and breath for the proletarian movement.*[12]

The cruel and unsparing, but needed, criticism that Cedric Johnson provides, particularly of ostensibly progressive forces like Black Lives Matter, is exactly what we need if we are to avoid the mistakes of the past and confront the barbarians at the gates today.

4

In Defense of Black Sentiment: A Comment on Cedric Johnson's Essay Re: Black Power Nostalgia

Mia White

> Now to talk to me about black studies as if it's something that concerned black people is an utter denial. This is the history of Western civilization.
>
> C.L.R. James[1]

A formidable and respected scholar at the University of Illinois-Chicago, Cedric Johnson has written an important essay, "The Panthers Can't Save Us Now." Johnson is adamant about the need to strongly and collectively advance left social justice demands in a political context that is starved of "the popular power needed to end the policing crisis." The author wants those of us in the United States to grapple with the challenge of mobilizing substantial numbers so as to be a significant enough force to effect "concrete political gains" in an era of neoliberalized power. In particular, Johnson is concerned that "Black Power militancy and nostalgia" (as perpetuated by the "digital afterlife of

movement imagery") and the related "Black ethnic essentialism," such as the author locates in contemporary Black
Lives Matter (BLM) activism, forestall the development of
broad, interracial coalitions that can together create lasting
social change. For Johnson, race- or identity-based political
organizing belies the cultural and class diversity of Black
America. Johnson points out that those with proximity to
power opportunistically use identity-based politics for their
own gains, building a conservative "elite-driven" Black-
professional-managerial class that profits from a patron-
client "bourgeois class politics." The production of this kind
of "Black exceptionalism" co-constructs what Johnson
frames as "commercial Keynesianism," and he posits that
these are practices that doom working-class solidarity across
ethno-racial lines because there is a tendency to "see urban
black life as fundamentally distinct from that of whites."
Johnson's standard for critique is whether we are moving
closer to "achieving concrete, substantive reform that might
curtail police violence and ensure greater democratic
accountability." For these reasons, Johnson posits that Black
ethnic politics "forestalls honest conversations about the real
class interests dominating today's neoliberal urban landscape." In response, the author wants us to prioritize a
"class-centered politics."

It has been somewhat difficult to figure out how to feel
about the positions Johnson takes in his important piece—
positions that I can gather many people have and perhaps do
not speak openly about, and positions I respect. The difficulty is partly because we are both Black people in academia

(I am a mixed Black woman of African American and immigrant Korean heritage), and for me our Blackness matters in the sense that these ambiguously overlapping histories make a feeling in my speech and in my mind—something of a contradiction perhaps to what the author is asking for. He in fact asks the reader not to pivot on certain ethnically motivated political affiliations (for the purposes of sustained social change) lest we lose our class-conscious focus, and yet I find myself thinking about Black study (a condition of possibility)[2] as I write and respond here, specifically about the ways Blackness is constructed in the arguments presented and how that matters. Wherever the differences in approach lie, I believe we need Johnson's perspective just as much as we need loving resistance to it. To address some of the author's concerns I offer the following.

We can agree that "racial identity" as a given set of universally held and experienced ideas may not exist (or may be a series of dream-killing enclosures), and we can agree that as a concept, it fails to grasp and attend to the galactic expression of Black diasporic experience that the author points to. In this vein, "race" requires clarity. Alexander Weheliye's straightforward formulation for race is helpful:

> Race should be viewed not as an ideology or the erroneous ascription of social meaning to existent biological classifications . . . but, in the words of Dorothy Roberts, as "a political system that governs people by sorting them into social groupings based on invented biological demarcations . . . Race is not a biological category that is

politically charged. It is a political category that has been disguised as a biological one."[3]

Operationally, race is "an ongoing set of political relations that require, through constant perpetuation via institutions, discourses, practices, desires, infrastructures, languages, technologies, sciences, economies, dreams, and cultural artifacts, the barring of nonwhite subjects from the category of the human as it is performed in the modern west."[4] This system produces racism as defined by Ruth Wilson Gilmore as premature vulnerability to state-sanctioned violence, functioning on different scales simultaneously—body, city, state, memory, and territory—and justified by race-based common sense.[5]

Thus, race as an assemblage (where race, location, and time together inform what it means to be human)[6] produces certain expressions of "Black ethnic politics," and though these expressions might represent a complex and evolving Pandora's box, we know for certain that Black identification processes far predate the BLM movement, and that they exist as a source of survival and support against a violent modern humanity committed to a "race" system (which, of course, includes white people). What I suggest with these ideas is that a truly "interracial" landscape of working-class solidarity with white people is most deeply possible through and with Black study, with a naked focus on race. If we thought about race in the manner of Sylvia Wynter, Katherine McKittrick, and Weheliye, there would be no way to circumvent capitalism, genocide, and immigrant and migrant dispossession. There would be no way to exclude white people. This would address our need for a more syncretic narrative of practical history, one which is found for example in the work of Lisa Lowe, where she "investigates the often obscured connections between the emergence of European liberalism, settler colonialism in the Americas, the transatlantic slave trade, and the east Indies and China trades in the late eighteenth and nineteenth centuries."[7] In a similar effort, George Ciccariello-Maher explores the need for a radical dialectical politics, writing that "for those relegated to nonbeing and condemned to invisibility, to even appear is a violent act—because it is violent to the structures of the world and because it will inevitably be treated as such."[8] Thus, these scholars suggest that concrete resistance requires we avoid "ontological apartheid" (the impulse to rank and make commensurate our histories and emplaced experiences). Intimacy would require that we deny the divisibility of class from race and gender (where one must become the standpoint through which the others are subsumed), in order to engage in a dialectical tension that keeps our solidarities stretching and unfinished.

Johnson develops a critique that the Black Panther Party movement (BPPM) failed to marshal broad-based support on the level of the New Deal, as an example of a universal program purported to have helped everyone. Yet the New Deal is widely critiqued for failing Black people,[9] specifically because most New Deal programs discriminated against Blacks, authorized separate and lower pay scales for Blacks, refused outright to support Black applicants (for example, the Federal Housing Authority refused to guarantee mortgages for Blacks who tried to buy in white neighborhoods), and the Civilian Conservation Corps maintained segregated camps. The Social Security Act excluded those job categories Blacks traditionally filled (domestic work), and the Agricultural Adjustment Administration policies forced more than 100,000 Blacks off the land in 1933 and 1934. At the same time, there was widespread working-class nonsupport for an anti-lynching bill and a bill to abolish the poll tax.

We could posit that it would be difficult to name a movement (including the BPPM) that was or is not limited in scope, scale, and purpose, and that we could reframe our understanding of the impact of movements to continue learning from them. A counterdiscourse would be one that admitted we do not always understand, or could not always have understood, a movement's shaping forces. "It is not possible," Ciccariello-Maher writes,

> to decolonize without radicalizing. Any process of decolonization that shies away from incessant dialectical tensions, the contingency of struggle, and the indeterminacy of the future risks reiterating the history of actually existing decolonization that Fanon unceremoniously dismissed as the "dead end" and "sterile formalism" of bourgeois nationalist rule.[10]

However, specific to the BPPM, it does bear noting that in fact this movement did produce the sort of tangible policy outcomes Johnson finds most compelling[11]—notably the nationwide adoption of the Black Panther Party's free breakfast programs. Nik Heynen investigates "how the BPP's Free Breakfast for Children Program was used as a political program for ensuring survival and social reproduction, but also how it was central to a dynamic rendering of utopian politics around the black Community" (our own Pandora's box), finding that

> the ways in which the BPP struggled for social reproduction through their breakfast program in their black communities, and how it allowed them to organize chapters across the United States, and then produce an internationally recognized moment of revolutionary potential, exhibits how individual actors transform and reproduce the material foundations of life in scaled ways, and transform the geographies of survival.[12]

Alondra Nelson finds that the BPP led the first nationally organized breakfast program in the United States, either in the public or private sector, and that the party's focus on health care was ideological, proceeding from the idea that Black people's access to health was a basic human right.[13]

Johnson speaks of a "mystification" whereby an adherence to "racial standpoint epistemology" (BLM providing a key example, per the author) obscures the "differing and conflicting material interests and ideological positions that animate black political life in real time and space," yet he requires his Black readers take up this very same elision in order to prioritize "working-class interests" before commitments to the divisive Black ethnic politics he outlines. This seems like a double

mystification that requires a second sight that is not recipro-
cated (the terms of which Du Bois spoke of with "double
consciousness" in *The Souls of Black Folk*), one in which Black
Americans in fact have historically engaged every midterm
and general election. Much has been made of the very durable
trend of Black women voters (followed by Black male voters)
overwhelmingly aligning with the Democratic Party up and
down midterm and general election tickets. These are the most
predictable Democratic voters in the United States, and they
already and loyally vote with a diverse, white-led political
party that purports to be about the people but falls victim to its
"neutrality" and to neoliberal capital pranks on a regular basis.
In other words, there is little evidence that Black voters are not
already doing what Johnson ask they do, because when Black
folks are overwhelmingly voting Democratic, they are not
voting with a Black Power sentiment—they are voting to make
the best decision possible under conditions of heteropatriar-
chal, capitalist, imperial white supremacy. We are still where
we are, surveilled and killed while walking, breathing, doing
our jobs, leaving on vacation, visiting friends, or driving a car.
Thus, to ask Black readers to shrug off race as a central analytic
is to ask them (1) to do what they already do on a regular basis
to survive as good liberal subjects, as if they don't; and (2) to
pretend that the very reason survival is so fraught has nothing
to do with the same reason we are ignored as an electorate. As
Alana Lentin states, "If the function of race is to determine the
boundaries of who is considered human and who is at its
borders (not-quite-human) or indeed, completely outside
(nonhuman), then any attempt to theorize race without placing

centrally the thoughts and experiences of those precisely defined as not-quite and nonhuman reenacts a racializing violence."[14]

Finally, on this point we might also ask ourselves whether in public life we could ever make similar political demands of indigenous North Americans, or any indigenous group, without risking real incredulity from even the most cynical *Fox News* pundit. It likely surprises no one, for instance, to hear that indigenous tribes living in the Amazon rain forest are protesting (on the basis of eco-*genocide*) Brazilian president-elect Jair Bolsonaro's public commitments to state-sponsored violence and neocolonial dispossession. On what basis could we suggest that their problems lie in their militancy (as Johnson suggests with regard to BPPM and BLM)? In the North American indigenous context, we know that "Indians" were often consolidated onto multi-tribe "reservation" enclosures, speaking different languages and having distinct geographical and cultural ways of knowing, and yet despite these diversities and diasporas, nonindigenous audiences witness a simultaneous, ongoing demand that indigenous cosmologies, treaties, and lives be reckoned with.

Black Solidarity: Politics, Not Biology

At the end of his magisterial book *We Who Are Dark* (2009), Tommie Shelby chooses to quote W.E.B. Du Bois's thinking and feeling from *Dusk of Dawn* (1940), where Du Bois examines a kind of "pragmatic nationalism" (not related to the nation-state):

But one thing is sure and that is the fact that since the fifteenth century these ancestors of mine and their other descendants have had a common history, have suffered a common disaster, and have one long memory. The actual ties of heritage between the individuals of this group vary with the ancestors that they have in common and many others: Europeans and Semites, perhaps Mongolians, certainly American Indians. But the physical bond is least and the badge of color relatively unimportant save as a badge; the real essence of this kinship is its social heritage of slavery, the discrimination and insult, and this heritage binds together not simply the children of Africa, but extends through yellow Asia and into the South Seas. It is this unity that draws me to Africa.[15]

Shelby uses this excerpt as a foundation for two related positions: (1) that Black political solidarity as understood through the common experience of racial oppression (one's vulnerability to anti-Black racism) continues to be a valuable source of motivation and strength in the face of unrelenting vulnerabilities, death, alienation, despair, and self-doubt—and toward a vigor "necessary for both self-respect and collective self-defense"; and (2) that a more robust solidarity must include a "specifically political mode of blackness practiced through certain principles such as anti-racism, equal educational and employment opportunity, and tolerance for group differences and individuality, and to emancipatory goals, such as achieving substantive racial equality—especially in employment, education, and wealth—and ending ghetto poverty."[16] Interestingly,

Shelby explicitly calls for Blacks to resist political centraliza-
tion, for the very reasons Johnson points to, and says Black
self-organization is important, should be voluntary, and should
be rooted in particular communities of interest—a multi-sited
public sphere focused on dialogue and participation. In this
sense, while Black interests can be advanced through multiracial associations or within a multiracial polity, the well-being of
Blacks always also requires—as a means to attend to accumulating, historical, unfair disadvantage—a collective sense of
Black self-determination.

   Johnson critiques "the liberal decoupling of race and class
that supplanted more radical versions of working-class left
politics," citing the BLM and the BPP movements as examples of why focusing on race is misguided and critiquing
these movements for a lack of outcomes. We can agree that
the decoupling is a problem, but it is a problem because race-
class is an always-present (and often ignored) intersectional
assemblage, present whether or not the guise is a focus on
"class consciousness." The influence of these movements
cannot be measured only in static outcomes (although there
are in fact real outcomes, such as the federal free breakfast
program and a deeper public tension and engagement with
Black vulnerability to "premature death").[17] The benefits of
universal programs such as the New Deal cannot be misremembered as materially transforming for the better the lives
of the most marginalized Black Americans. Continued deep
grappling with race and white supremacy by Black Americans
can help us cultivate a Black political consciousness and solidarity from which to strengthen race-class articulations,

whereas the pivot to support class political interests along party lines with the kind of power and influence Johnson seeks has not demonstrated to Black Americans the kinds of mutuality and support required in an ongoing, historically and cumulatively race-class reality.

5

Black Exceptionalism and the Militant Capitulation to Economic Inequality

Touré Reed

Cedric Johnson's "The Panthers Can't Save Us Now" is a compelling, historically grounded critique of contemporary anti-racist campaigns against police brutality and mass incarceration. While Johnson is encouraged by the swell of organized opposition to the carceral state and to the vigilantism precipitated by the murder of Trayvon Martin, he is pessimistic about the capacity of groups such as Black Lives Matter to deliver on comprehensive prison reform. Specifically, Johnson contends that BLM's insistence on viewing the carceral state through the lens of "black exceptionalism" has produced narrow demands for race-specific remedies to problems—such as police violence, hyperincarceration, and income inequality—that are rooted in political-economic processes that transcend race. Johnson traces this tendency, in part, to "a prevailing nostalgia for Black Power militancy" that has encouraged "continued pursuit of modes of black ethnic politics." Identifying the vindicationist bent of recent scholarship on Black Power as a major source of the appeal of disparitarian critiques of hyperincarceration and inequality, Johnson challenges "black exceptionalism" by detailing the framework's origins as well as its inadequacies.

Johnson convincingly argues that the centrality of identitarianism to contemporary activist and scholarly critiques of mass incarceration and income inequality not only obscures the political-economic roots of what we tend to call racial disparities but also encourages counter-solidaristic politics. Nonblacks, as Johnson notes, comprise the majority of both the inmate population and those murdered by police officers. Yet legal scholar Michelle Alexander's commitment to viewing the current era of hyperincarceration through the anachronistic lens of Jim Crow has led her to cast nonblack inmates—who comprise 60 percent of the total incarcerated population—as "collateral damage." Similarly, even as whites accounted for nearly 40 percent of Flint residents poisoned by Michigan Republican governor Rick Snyder and former Flint city manager Darnell Earley, activists, scholars, and even presidential candidate Hillary Clinton decried this man-made tragedy as evidence of systemic racism, implying, whatever their intent, that Flint's nonblack residents either deserved their fate or were beside the point. As Johnson forcefully argues, the carceral state was not birthed simply of white racism—even if racism is among the issues informing profiling and sentencing disparities—but rather, zero tolerance policing and hyperincarceration function as mechanisms for dispatching late-stage capitalism's surplus population, whatever their race. Snyder's and Earley's sociopathic actions were, likewise, part and parcel of the neoliberal governor's broader assault on the public sector and on poor and work-ing-class people.[1]

While liberal disparitarians' tendency toward theoretical or metaphorical abstractions often obscures the ugly class politics to which ethnic exceptionalism is frequently bound, neoliberal technocrats' disregard for poor and working-class people of all races is transparent. Just ahead of the 2016 Republican primaries, pundit Fareed Zakaria published an op-ed titled "America's Self-Destructive Whites," which laid bare neoliberal identitarianism's counter-solidaristic and inhumane conclusions. Zakaria attributed the soaring rates of suicide among middle-aged, working-class whites to a collec-tive sense of entitlement—or what some might term "white privilege." Treating neoliberalism's contribution to "white working-class" despair as simply the product of a rationally functioning market, Zakaria dismissed economic malaise as the culprit via comparison with African Americans and Latinos—compatriots who "face greater economic pressure than whites." Since blacks' and Hispanics' mortality rates had actually declined over the past few decades, Zakaria reasoned that after hundreds of years of slavery, Jim Crow, and racism, African Americans "developed ways to cope with disappoint-ment and the unfairness of life: through family, art, protest speech, and, above all, religion."[2]

Operating as if the objects of his contempt had been divested of the franchise, Zakaria described working-class whites as "an elite group" who had once been "central to America's economy, its society . . . [and] its very identity," but whose time has since passed. Zakaria went on to assert that Donald Trump had promised to restore their former greatness and then chastened Trump's working-class white supporters for their delusional embrace of the real estate mogul's pitch.[3]

Some may be unfazed by Zakaria's contempt for working-class white Trump supporters; however, the implications of his characterization of African Americans are no less callous. Indeed, Zakaria not only held up blacks as role models for lowered expectations in the age of neoliberalism but did so through a narrative of African American exceptionalism. In his unintentionally ironic case for religion as the opiate of the black masses, for example, Zakaria described Martin Luther King Jr.'s "I Have a Dream" speech as an example of African Americans' acceptance of suffering as their lot in life.[4] Of course, Zakaria made no mention of the fact that King and the organizers of the 1963 March on Washington for Jobs and Freedom—black labor leaders A. Philip Randolph and Bayard Rustin—had demanded a more expansive role for government in the nation's economic affairs with the end of opening pathways, for blacks and even poor whites, to the stable working class. Zakaria's reflections on the so-called white working-class elite, likewise, ignore the fact that blacks have long been overrepresented among union members. Unionized black workers earn higher wages, are more likely to have pensions and health insurance, and are less likely to experience a racial wage gap than are their nonunion counterparts. Blacks have therefore been hit harder by the decline of the manufacturing sector and the neoliberal assault on the public sector than have whites.[5]

A staunch opponent of progressive redistributive policies in the United States and around the globe, Zakaria's neoliberal agenda could not accommodate such historicist interpretations of black life. Instead, "identitarianism" allowed Zakaria to see blacks as noble, long-suffering victims of ontological racism rather than of economic processes, while neoliberalism's "entitled" white losers were simply getting their comeuppance.

BLM's *Vision for Black Lives* proposed the kind of egalitarian agenda that is anathema to the likes of Zakaria. Still, according to Johnson, BLM's embrace of "black exceptionalism" has led activists to understate the impact of issues like automation, the decline of unionization, deregulation, and public sector retrenchment on the plight of blacks and other working people. And while the *Vision for Black Lives* attempted to broaden BLM's scope, Johnson argues that its commitment to ethnic group politics—which, among other things, presumes that shared racial status can bind black leftists, liberals, and conservatives in common cause—undercuts activists' capacity to mobilize a broad constituency, motivated by common interest, for either police reform or income equality.

Johnson ultimately traces the appeal to contemporary activists of black exceptionalism, in part, to popular conceptions of Black Power, which have failed to take stock of either the movement's origins or its actual political legacy.

Black Power, according to Johnson, reflected a conservative turn in postwar liberal politics. The decline of left-labor militancy during the Cold War combined with a growing spatial divide between working-class whites and poor and working-class African Americans to engender a postwar liberal discourse that—in contrast to New Deal liberalism—uncoupled inequality from political economy. By the 1960s, this tendency would lead Democratic policymakers to devise an inadequate War on Poverty centered on the combination of growth initiatives and race-specific remedies. The Great Society's War on Poverty on the cheap predictably failed to eliminate the root causes of racial disparities; however, Johnson makes clear that not only did programs like Job Corps, Community Action Program (CAP), Volunteers in Service to America (VISTA), and Model Cities nurture a nascent black professional middle class, but CAP's "maximum feasible participation" encouraged urban African American activists to embrace a vision of democracy rooted in ethnic pluralism and racial group authenticity.

The reactionary implications of Black Power's ethnic pluralist framework were plain to the movement's contemporary left critics. Bayard Rustin—a critic of both Black Power and the War on Poverty—noted, in 1966, that the growing tide of cultural nationalism aided and abetted an anemic War on Poverty. According to Rustin, Black Power's embrace of ethnic-group succession diminished both the government's and the union movement's indispensable contributions to white ethnics' ascendancy from tenements to suburbs. In other words, black cultural nationalists' Moynihan-like tendency to attribute white ethnics' economic mobility to group culture rather than, say, the National Labor Relations Act and the Federal Housing Act was not only wrong but also validated the War on Poverty's rejection of the kind of interventionist policies that had, in fact, improved the material lives of millions of white workers from the New Deal through the 1960s. Rustin ultimately warned that Black Power's emphasis on racial-group representation would serve the interests of an aspirant African American political and managerial class at the expense of the vast majority of poor and working-class blacks. Identifying automation and the deindustrialization of American cities, rather than white supremacy, as the principal culprits, Rustin insisted that race-specific remedies were incapable of redressing racial disparities. Instead, he, A. Philip Randolph, and economist Leon Keyserling proposed the *Freedom Budget*, which—like the failed Full Employment Bill of 1945—would have mandated a living wage and guaranteed public sector employment to the nation's unemployed.[6]

Rustin, Randolph, and Keyserling's *Freedom Budget* was not to pass, as neither the War on Poverty nor Black Power could accommodate the type of class-based politics that they and other labor liberals believed was essential to redressing 1960s-era disparities. By the 1970s, however, the political training that War on Poverty initiatives like CAP provided Black Power "radicals" helped usher in the first wave of black elected officials since Reconstruction. According to Johnson, many of the black urban regimes of the seventies and early eighties addressed their black constituencies' concerns about police brutality. But with the War on Drugs, black officials threw in with draconian policing—pressured not just by the federal government, but by *black* constituencies in high-crime neighborhoods in cities rocked by deindustrialization.

In the wake of the 2016 presidential election, the value of Cedric Johnson's important article is clear. The Clinton campaign successfully used identitarianism to counter a Sanders insurgency that traced disparities to a quarter century of bipartisan commitment to neoliberalism. Clinton's efforts to use this tactic to both push back left critics and woo black voters may have been more transparently opportunistic than the Lyndon B. Johnson administration's efforts to co-opt Black Power militants; nevertheless, both tactics diverted attention from the political-economic roots of disparities and undercut the prospects for a better politics for disproportionately black and brown poor and working-class people. While some have taken Donald Trump's successful use of white identity politics, also known as white nationalism, as proof of race's realness and racism's permanence, Trump's cabinet and Supreme Court appointments make clear that his presidency—which will likely usher in a return to Lochner-era labor and regulatory laws—does not bode well for *anyone* who works for a living. Indeed, even if Trump's regular vilification of black and brown people ensures that the horrific implications of his presidency are clearest for people of color, his Supreme Court picks will deal major blows to not just anti-discrimination laws and abortion rights, but the right to collective bargaining, protections from employer coercion and caprice, environmental protections, food and drug safety, and more. When read in the full context of the past half century of American politics, then, the crucial takeaway from Johnson's trenchant analysis of Black Power thinking is that when it comes to identity politics, fighting fire with fire only ensures that poor and working people—a grouping that encompasses most people of color—will get burned, while capital warms itself in the glow of victory.

6

Cedric Johnson and the Other Sixties' Nostalgia

Kim Moody

There is something politically familiar in Cedric Johnson's two essays in *Catalyst* and *New Politics*.[1] Because his political conclusions are very general, even vague—ones that build "on broad solidarity around commonly felt needs and interest" . . . by "building alliances not on identity as such, but on shared values and demonstrated commitments"—it is difficult to put one's finger on just what the precise political and social conclusions of his essays are.[2] Yet, despite the rejection of sixties' nostalgia, the elegance of the language, and the contemporary originality of his arguments and supporting evidence, there is the ring in Johnson's two essays of a familiar sixties' politics that sought to be the alternative, first, to militancy in the movement, and later, to Black Power "back in the day."

This was a politics that downplayed the significance of race as a dividing line in working-class life and American society in general without denying the reality of racism in the aftermath of the passage of the Civil Rights Act in 1964.

Simultaneously, it substituted the trade union bureaucracy for the working class in the practice of "building alliances" in its version of "coalition politics." It was associated above all with A. Philip Randolph and Bayard Rustin, two of the best-known African Americans in this country's civil rights, labor, and socialist movements. These important figures are mentioned not only in Johnson's *Catalyst* essay, but by Touré Reed as well, in his *New Politics* contribution[3]—though only in the post–Civil Rights Act phase of their political careers. Indeed, I have recently run across this reference to Rustin and the sixties a number of times in the ongoing debate over the relevance and weight of race and class in left political analysis and practice. I will return to this below.

Much of what Johnson says about the failures of Black Power and the cross-class nature of Black America then and now is true and has been analyzed by others such as Manning Marable, among many.[4] Johnson's arguments are, of course, more up to date. I will not attempt to present a different analysis of "black exceptionalism," as he calls it, but rather an analysis of Johnson's implied political direction—what I will call "the other" sixties nostalgia. But first, a look at the reality of "hyperincarceration" on which much of his argument is based.

Locking Up by Class and Race

The criminal "justice" system has always been a class project under capitalism with its central foundation of exclusive private property and the need to protect it. This is as true in countries that historically have had no significant racial minorities as in those that did. Indeed, in the case of the United States, if the criminal "justice" system did not lock up offending or misbehaving white people, it would be of little use to capital. At the same time, of course, it is very selective of which white people are most likely to be arrested, tried and incarcerated. Misbehaving bankers who ruin the lives of millions by breaking or bending the law are more likely to get a bonus than a sentence, while white working-class offenders who rob or harm individuals or small businesses get the slammer. Case closed? It might be if the working class of the United States was not so racially diverse, structurally unequal, locked out of whatever channels of upward mobility there once were, and forced to compete with itself for jobs, housing, education, and much else even more intensely than in the pre-neoliberal era. Just who, then, gets incarcerated in the United States?

First, it is important to distinguish between prison and jail.[5] Those in jail account for about a quarter of all those incarcerated at about 740,000 in 2016. The incarceration rate (inmates per 100,000 US residents) in jail for blacks was three and a half times that for "non-Hispanic" whites, while that of (nonwhite) Latinos was 50 percent greater. This is already a sure sign of unequal treatment given that non-Hispanic whites compose 60 percent of the US population, blacks 13 percent, and Latinos 18 percent, with the rest mostly other people of color and a small number not identified by race. But jail is not the heart of today's carceral state. Over half (55 percent) the jail population turns over every week, and the average stay is twenty-five days. At the heart of hyperincarceration are the federal and state prisons where those sentenced do "hard time," with the average stay in a state prison running two and a half years. It is here, too, that in thirty-two states the death penalty applies.

The table opposite shows the prison population for 2016. What we see is a wildly disproportionate representation of blacks, Latinos, and other people of color, composing together almost 70 percent of the prison population. Behind this disproportion lies the highly discriminatory practice of sentencing. Here blacks are almost six times and Latinos three times more likely to be sentenced to "hard time" in prison than whites. These disproportions have been increased somewhat by the introduction in the last twenty years of algorithms for the targeting of police operations, such as PredPol, and sentencing, such as LSI-R, which are widely used across the United States. These probability-based algorithms not only incorporate the (mostly unconscious) biases of their designers and programmers but, worse still, create mathematical feedback loops that increase the targeting of black neighborhoods and hence underplay the frequency of similar crimes in white neighborhoods. The same biased feedback loops operate in sentencing algorithms. So, while non-Hispanic whites were 34 percent of prison inmates in 2006, they were down to 30 percent a decade later. Note here that no one involved in the digitalization of criminal "justice" was required to be a raving racist, believer in white supremacy, to have voted for Donald Trump, or even necessarily to be white. The racial bias had been built into the system long ago—the "blind" administration—and now technology was sufficient to perpetuate and even intensify racial bias.

Population of Federal and State Prisons by Race and Ethnicity, 2016

Race	Population	Percentage
Total	1,459,533	100
Non-Hispanic White	440,200	30
Black	487,300	33
Latino	339,600	23
Other*	192,433	16

* Mostly Native Americans, Pacific Islanders, Asians, and a small number of those not designated by race.
Source: *US Department of Justice, Bureau of Justice Statistics (2018)*, "Prisoners in 2016."

That these figures are in part the result of the War on Drugs, zero tolerance policies as well as "broken windows" law enforcement is true enough. That black middle-class professionals and politicians played a contradictory and even reactionary role in demanding or developing these policies, as Johnson argues, is undeniable—although it is most certainly a subordinate role in terms of federal and state policy and practice. Indeed, whether in the old ghetto or today's leafy black neighborhoods, the black middle class and petty bourgeoisie have always played a contradictory role in the long struggle for black freedom. None of this refutes the existence of either underlying structures of racial inequality or the practice of racism in the criminal "justice" system, as countless studies have shown. It is also the case, as Johnson points out, that black working-class people in today's black "exclusive class zone" have demanded the police protection they are routinely denied.[6] Given the outsized presence of the police in stop and frisk, drug sweeps, the deployment of militarized SWAT teams, and other operations in poor black neighborhoods, this itself is quite a comment on the racially selective class nature of policing today. Stopping, frisking, harassing, arresting and incarcerating disproportionate numbers of black males is not the same thing as providing protection to the majority of black residents.

The escalation of incarceration is not simply a matter of controlling the "surplus population," as Johnson argues. It is, as I stated above, a class project, but one with racist assumptions and practices. Those who are sentenced to prison are not primarily from the "surplus population." In fact, nearly two-thirds of the prison population were employed prior to incarceration. Forty-nine percent of all prisoners were employed full-time and another 16 percent in part-time work before entering prison, while another 8 percent were students, retired, or permanently disabled, according to a study by the National Center for Education Statistics. To be sure, many of these jobs would have been poorly paid, and some who held them had probably moved in and out of the labor force, but only 19 percent of prisoners in 2014 were unemployed at the time of incarceration. Johnson's inclusion of low-paid workers in the "surplus population" or reserve army of labor dismisses its functions in capital accumulation and becomes too broad a group to have much meaning.

The functions of the "surplus population" or reserve army of labor is to depress wages by increasing competition, as Johnson points out, but also to provide a pool of available workers to fill the entry slots in new or growing industries in accordance with the needs of capital accumulation. Today, this would include industries such as health care, hospitality, food service, and warehousing, among others. To fulfill these tasks, those in the reserve army must be either unemployed, between jobs, or "not in the labor force" (including women doing family care). Some students and retired people can fill in part-time jobs as well. If employed workers were counted as part of the reserve army, however, the 28 percent of those employed who earn below the poverty line, or possibly the 30 percent of the workforce that draws on some form of government aid in order to get by (percentages that would be significantly larger if only working-class employees were counted), would be included along with the millions of unemployed and those "not in the labor force" or marginally attached to it, and the concept would be a useless analytical tool.

The conclusion that race and racism are major factors in determining who does "hard time" in prison, just as they strongly influence who gets the worst jobs and who faces racial harassment and even violence on the job (no matter what it pays), is simply unavoidable. Each year, some 90,000 cases are filed with the Equal Employment Opportunity Commission (EEOC), the majority of which deal with race and mostly come from employed workers. This does not include court cases, grievances filed over racial harassment or discrimination, or the countless numbers of those in employment who suffer in silence. Johnson is right that Jim Crow is not an apt name for the subjective, structural, institutional, material, and political forms and underpinnings of racism as they have evolved since the civil rights era and deepened with the advent of neoliberalism. But race, unscientific category that it is, remains a major basis, cutting across class, for sorting out of who gets what in American society. To reject this reality is not to adopt a class perspective, but on the contrary to reject the working class of this country in all its actually existing inequality, diversity, and increased competition.

The "Other" Sixties Nostalgia; or, Choosing the Wrong Randolph and Rustin

As noted above, Johnson and a growing number of others who favor what they believe is a class orientation and reject "identity politics" have referred to the political direction proposed by Bayard Rustin and A. Philip Randolph in the mid-1960s—what I call the "other" sixties nostalgia. Both are important figures in US history, and their politics deserve review. The problem here is that their politics changed in important ways at a crucial point in the development of the long black freedom struggle, and neither their previous views on black self-organization nor the cross-class direction they proposed in the wake of the passage of the Civil Rights Act receive the attention they require by those who cite their post-1964 coalition politics. In light of the debate on race and class today, we need to look at their views on both black self-organization and coalition politics as they evolved.

Randolph was a self-proclaimed socialist and a long-standing advocate and practitioner of black self-organization that frequently excluded whites and put forth demands relating specifically to blacks, as well as a believer in working-class solidarity and advancement. The Brotherhood of Sleeping Car Porters and Maids was an entirely black union, though one supposes if there had been any white porters or maids (a very unlikely possibility at that time) they could have joined the union. When Randolph organized the first March on Washington Movement in 1941 (with Rustin's aid) to demand black jobs in the nation's growing defense industries, however, he insisted that it be an "all-black" movement that excluded even white supporters. In announcing the planned march Randolph stated: "On to Washington, ten thousand black Americans . . . We will not call on our white friends to march with us. There are some things Negroes must do alone. This is our fight and we must see it through."[7]

To the disappointment of many, the march scheduled for July 1, 1941, was canceled when Franklin D. Roosevelt signed Executive Order 8802 establishing a "fair employment practices committee" to prevent discrimination in defense and government employment. Many felt 8802 was inadequate.

In the 1950s, Randolph organized the Negro American Labor Council, again an exclusively black organization, to fight specifically for the rights of black workers in the labor movement. The NALC was itself an umbrella organization of black caucuses that existed throughout the labor movement long before anyone had spoken of "black power," much less "identity politics." This included black caucuses in industrial unions such as the United Auto Workers and the United Steel Workers where, in both cases, blacks were largely excluded from skilled trades jobs despite (or because of?) the liberalism of the unions' leaders.

Randolph and the NALC did constant battle throughout the late 1950s and early '60s, not only with George Meany and the exclusionary building trade unions, but with liberals and the social democratic leaders of the garment unions as well. He was routinely attacked as undermining class solidarity, advocating dual unionism, and practicing "racism in reverse." To these charges Rustin, then an aid to Randolph, replied in 1961, "Under present conditions—i.e., general segregation and discrimination, and the unreliability of today's organized (or disorganized) liberalism—the Negro finds it necessary in many instances to organize independently." Was this "identity politics" without the label? Or was it the recognition that in the struggle for black freedom and equality, black self-organization was an indispensable tool, even (or perhaps particularly) where unity and solidarity with whites was (as in the labor movement) expected but often denied?

Less than four years later, Rustin was singing a different tune in his influential essay "From Protest to Politics," published in February 1965 in *Commentary* as well as in the subsequent articles cited by Johnson. In all of these Rustin argued for the strategy known as "realignment" already advocated by some socialists, notably Michael Harrington. The vehicle for and object of this realignment was, of course, the Democratic Party. As Rustin put it in the 1965 essay:

The future of the Negro struggle depends in whether the contradictions of this society can be resolved by a coalition of progressive forces which becomes the *effective* political majority in the United States. I speak of the coalition which staged the March on Washington, passed the Civil Right Act, and laid the basis for the Johnson landslide—Negroes, trade unionists, liberals, and religious groups.[8]

Apparently, by that time the liberals, including yesterday's discriminating white labor leaders, had become "dependable." In fact, the coalition Rustin described had already begun its disintegration as the movement reached a crossroads spurred by the dramatic events of 1964. These included the explosive campaign led by Martin Luther King Jr. and its repression in Birmingham, Alabama; the first of the urban riots in Harlem; the passage of the Civil Rights Act; and the rejection of the Mississippi Freedom Democratic Party (MFDP) at the Democratic National Convention at the hands of not only Lyndon B. Johnson, but the very liberals and union leaders who were supposed to be the major elements in this "coalition of progressive forces" that Rustin, Harrington, and others saw as the key to realignment. In "From Protest to Politics" Rustin defends the "compromise" offered the MFDP delegates as a victory.

Realignment as an electoral strategy was always a top-down project in which liberal office holders and pressure group advocates in the Democratic Party dominated and labor leaders were the junior partners who substituted for the working class or even the union membership. "The politics of insider negotiation" Johnson says Rustin later developed were not an aberration in this version of coalition politics, but the modus operandi of the realignment strategy from the start.[9] This was a political method that led to an alliance not just with liberals but with none other than George Meany, the labor leader who refused to endorse the 1963 March on Washington, backed the 1964 rejection of the MFDP delegation, and with whom Randolph had crossed swords just a couple of years earlier. That, in turn, led Rustin to support the war in Vietnam and later to oppose affirmative action in the building trades. It was never a class orientation, but an effort to make one of the nation's preeminent cross-class, bourgeois-dominated institutions stand in for actual working-class political organization and even for a social democratic politics the Democratic Party was incapable of adopting.[10]

The rejection of the MFDP by Democratic bigwigs, liberals, and labor leaders and the humiliating "compromise" they offered the black delegation was central to the new direction Student Nonviolent Coordinating Committee activists, most visibly Stokely Carmichael, would take in the next couple of years. Though the slogan "Black Power" would not be publicly articulated by Carmichael or anyone else until the spring of 1966, the idea that the civil rights, nonviolent (or in Rustin's terms "protest") phase of the movement had reached its limits, and that deeper forms of power were needed to advance the interests of the black population, was becoming universal. Rustin proposed one version, Carmichael and others another, King still another a little later in the form of the Poor Peoples' Campaign that led to his fatal presence in support of the Memphis sanitation workers' strike. This latter direction being the closest to a genuine class politics.

The great irony of all of this is that by the late 1970s, all the currents in black and coalition politics, regardless of label or intention—the opportunist urban politicians, the "poverty pimps" of the short-lived War on Poverty and its community control aftermath, most of the Black Power (capital B, capital P) militants, and the top-down realigners—ended up in the same place: the Democratic Party. That is, the party that escalated the war in Vietnam, that began its long journey to the political center and beyond in the mid 1970s, abandoned urban aid in the 1980s in tandem with Reagan, ended "welfare as we know it" and escalated the carceral state under Clinton in the 1990s, and deeply disappointed those who believed "Yes We Can" under the neoliberal leadership of Barack Obama.

The unexpected, unprecedented 2016 campaign of Bernie Sanders for the Democratic presidential nomination, the growth of Democratic Socialists of America, and the 2018 election of democratic socialists Alexandria Ocasio-Cortez and Rashida Tlaib to the House of Representatives, along with a number of like-minded leftists to lesser offices (all as Democrats), have helped to revive the effort to move the Democratic Party to places it has never been. Among those places where it once was under pressure of a massive labor upsurge (now revived with a Green prefix), of course, was the other major source of social democratic nostalgia, the New Deal—the severe class and racial limits of which Dan La Botz and Mia White have pointed out.[11] This recent resurrection of "boring within" the Democratic Party, without the anachronistic "realignment" branding, to be sure, has been given even further encouragement by the apparent adoption of some left demands such a Medicare for All, federal jobs guarantees, and the Green New Deal, among others, by some of the candidates for the 2020 Democratic presidential nomination besides Bernie. The genuine threat and practice of the Trump administration adds fuel to this fire.

With this renewed hope has come a demotion of race as a subject of socioeconomic analysis in the name of class that is, in reality, a return to America's quintessential business-funded, neoliberal-dominated, undemocratic, cross-class social construction: the Democratic Party. As a Marxist who has put class at the center of my analyses over the years, I naturally believe it will take more than the efforts of black Americans, or even blacks and Latinos combined, to end economic and racial inequality. It will take a class-based movement and politics, with socialist politics at its center. But I also have seen both firsthand, through involvement in the civil rights and labor movements as well as through study and research, that embedded racism requires the self-organization of the oppressed to shape or supplement the broader programs in such a way that that they do not simply reproduce racial inequality in new, sometimes less visible forms, as they often have in the past—for instance, in the New Deal and the post–World War II GI Bill.

Among other things, the geographic reality of de facto segregation means substandard education, housing, food, and services for blacks, along with punitive welfare and policing operations. Medicare for All, a federal jobs guarantee, a decent minimal or living wage, and a Green New Deal are all things we must fight for and that would improve the lives of everyone. But as they fail to alter the geography of race and leave the delivery of services and the content of jobs in private/capitalist hands, racial and gender discrimination, harassment, and violence, along with unequal implementation, delivery, and administration, will remain embedded if not specifically rooted out. These "universal" programs also leave the harassment, bullying and violence that blacks experience in the workplace, "be their payment high or low," in the hands of managers who tolerate these even when they don't actually participate in them—hence the countless EEOC lawsuits filed each year. Liberals, social democrats, and even unions have repeatedly failed to address these consequences of racism when oppressed people have not fought militantly for such change or when they have been too poorly organized or too weak to enforce it.

The sixties failed to produce the sort of class-based politics and political organization capable of bringing serious social change. Nostalgia for that era cannot be a guide to the tasks of the present and future. As one who supported (and supports) the right of black self-organization and worked in coalition with the Panthers in Brooklyn in 1968 (a largely positive experience), I don't mind saying that this goes for the hope that something like the Black Panther Party will "save us now." But it also goes for the more active contemporary fantasy and alternative bit of nostalgia that coalescing in the Democratic Party will be the salvation for a left long in the wilderness but now growing again. This time, we need to take both class and race seriously.

7

What Black Life Actually Looks Like

Cedric Johnson

Since 2013, Black Lives Matter has served as a broad banner uniting citizens from all walks of life against the most egregious and visible use of police force against black civilians. Until the election of Donald Trump, who made his "Blue Lives Matter" commitments well known from the very moment he announced his candidacy,[1] popular demonstrations against police killings spread like prairie fires across the country, from Oakland to Ferguson and on to Baltimore, Chicago, Dallas, and Baton Rouge. As a rallying cry, "Black Lives Matter" opened up public space for disparate campaigns, networks of grieving families, criminal justice reform organizations, and localized struggles against the carceral state that had been in motion for decades.

At the same time, however, like most great slogans, "Black Lives Matter" advanced a rather straightforward, if not simplistic, analysis of the issue at hand: that the problems of policing were primarily racial. Black Lives Matter fervor also unleashed a torrent of historical misinformation, conspiracy theory, and wrongheaded thinking about politics. In elevating a race-centric interpretation of American life and history, Black Lives Matter has actually had the effect of making it more difficult to think critically and honestly about black life as it exists, in all of its complexity and contradictions. Rather than clearing a path through the thickets, some left intellectuals have made peace with this overgrowth of bad historical thinking, even though it threatens to choke out the possibility for cultivating the kind of critical left analyses of society we so desperately need.

Mia White's "In Defense of Black Sentiment"[2] offers criticism of my 2017 *Catalyst* essay "The Panthers Can't Save Us Now: Anti-Policing Struggles and the Limits of Black Power"; Kim Moody's "Cedric Johnson and the Other Sixties' Nostalgia" addresses that essay, and my more recent *New Politics* essay "Who's Afraid of Left Populism?" I appreciate that both White and Moody have taken time to craft responses to my work. I first came to know White as part of a growing, dedicated community of scholars researching the 2005 Hurricane Katrina disaster and the long process of reconstruction and recovery that followed. White's work stood out because of its focus on the Mississippi Gulf Coast, often neglected by the urban studies bias toward the plight of New Orleans. I've never met Moody, but during the aughts, when my economist colleague Chris Gunn and I routinely co-taught a labor course at Hobart and William Smith Colleges, Moody's writings on American working-class history were instrumental in shaping our approach to the course, and were a mainstay of our assigned readings. His 1997 book *Workers in a Lean World* was especially helpful for making sense of the painful impact of globalized production on the once-bustling manufacturing towns surrounding us in Western New York.

While I think we are all on the same side politically, and there are definite points of agreement between our essays, White and Moody rehearse some errant arguments about race, politics, and class power that have become orthodoxy on the contemporary left. In what follows, I want to contest some of their core claims regarding the character of black political life; the role of contemporary policing in managing surplus population, New Deal social democracy, and African American progress; and finally, the relationship between electoral politics, the Democratic Party, and the future of the American left.

Both authors abide some version of Black Lives Matter sensibility, sharing a suspicion of class-conscious politics as always reproducing racial disparities historically and into the future. My central contention with both White and Moody lies in their reluctance to engage in meaningful class analysis of black political life. Their use of clichés and anachronisms when addressing black life reflects a broader affliction of the contemporary left. This difficulty in discussing black life in a critical-historical manner filters out and contaminates interpretations of labor and capital, and ultimately undermines strategic political thinking.

At the start of his essay, Moody says that he "will not attempt to present a different analysis of 'black exceptionalism,' " but in fact, his and White's essays are both defenses of black exceptionalism, the very interpretative and discursive sensibility that I have criticized in recent writings. Black political life is and always has been heterogeneous, a complex of shifting ideological positions and competing interests. Black political life has always been shaped by broader conflicts between labor and capital, even in the contexts where black noncitizen or second-class-citizen status was the norm. When White and Moody turn to black political life, however, these basic empirical-historical facts of African American political development are minimized, or vanish altogether. This is not a new problem.

Black Life beyond the Barricades

In his 1962 essay "Revolutionary Nationalism and the Afro-American," Harold Cruse complained that "American Marxists cannot 'see' the Negro at all unless he is storming the barricades, either in the present or in history."[3] The World War II veteran and ex-Communist partisan put the matter even more bluntly, saying that American Marxists—his euphemism for his former party comrades—wrongly view blacks as "a people without classes or differing class interests." Cruse also denounced the falsehood of the "Negro Liberation Movement," a favored term of his left contemporaries, as an " 'all-class' affair united around a program of civil and political equality." I don't evoke Cruse here because I think he had all the answers to what ails us—the same is true for my discussion of Bayard Rustin below. Cruse is frustrated by the oversimplifications and occlusions of African American life and history he has witnessed within the

Communist Party. From this acknowledgment of a more complex, class-stratified world beyond the desks of Herbert Aptheker and his old Communist Party comrades, Cruse pivots toward a defense of a revolutionary black leadership. What he desires is that the black bourgeoisie act as a truly national bourgeoisie. Setting aside the problems of this argument, which Cruse would enlarge in his 1967 book *The Crisis of the Negro Intellectual*, his basic criticism of the left may be as insightful today as it was when he first wrote it.

In the age of Black Lives Matter protests, many activists and academics seem unable to see the complexity of black life beyond the barricades, or outside the frame of the latest viral video killing of a black civilian. Neither White nor Moody engage in much substantive discussion of actually existing black political life, the fact of differing black class interests, or the fundamental demographic and cultural changes within black life and American society of the last half century. While White attempts to marshal normative theory and autoethnography to build a case for a redemptive Black Power sensibility, Moody either explains away class conflict among blacks as inconsequential, or assumes the familiar, deferential posture of white New Leftists toward the "self-organization of the oppressed."

In both cases, their prose remains lodged in the literary conventions emerging from decades-gone social conditions. White's essay rehearses Black Power sentiment, the black population as a socially coherent and unified political constituency deriving from twentieth-century conditions of black ghettoization and Jim Crow segregation. Moody's essay, on the other hand, recalls New Left anxieties and attempts to navigate the spatial and cultural gulf between the mid-twentieth-century urban black ghetto and the expanding white suburban middle class and its deepening commitments to capitalism.

White employs the racial "we" to drive her analysis, and throughout she engages in a form of ventriloquism that has long been a problem within black political life and scholarly and popular interpretations thereof. "We are still where we are, surveilled and killed while walking, breathing, doing our jobs, leaving a vacation, visiting friends, or driving a car," White writes. "Thus, to ask Black readers to shrug off race as a central analytic is to ask them (1) to do what they already do on a regular basis to survive as good liberal subjects, as if they don't; and (2) to pretend that the very reason survival is so fraught has nothing to do with the same reason we are ignored as an electorate."

Aside from how the second half of her statement mischaracterizes the intent and conclusions of my argument, there are two immediate problems with this passage. First, while her use of the first-person plural has dramatic impact, it obscures the actual dynamics of police killings, advancing the falsehood that all blacks, regardless of class position, are equally likely to be victims of daily surveillance, harassment, detainment, and arrest. White abides the popular New Jim Crow accounting of the carceral state as fundamentally racist in motives and effects, but this is hyperbolic and misleading. Blacks are disproportionately represented among the victims of arrest-related incidents in most years since the start of this century, but blacks are not the majority of victims. As I argued in the 2017 *Catalyst* essay and recent *New Politics* essay, contemporary policing has a class character that is not reflected in viral videos, which only capture some police-civilian conflicts and are circulated through social media networks and practices that are governed by standing assumptions and ideological predispositions of users and their social and psychological needs, often at the expense of other evidence like national Justice Department statistics, killings undocumented by cell phone camera, and deaths that do not conform to the New Jim Crow frame. The blackness of the victims is visible, evocative, and foregrounded in popular understandings of why they were targeted; their common position among the most submerged elements of the working class is not as readily legible for some audiences.

Second, this use of the racial "we" preempts politics, and by that I am referring not simply to the arena of elections and party politics, as White implies, but to the broader contexts where social power is mobilized and contested. The very real diversity of black experiences and political sentiments of the carceral state are lost in White's essay, and in much Black Lives Matter discourse, both of which retreat into abstraction. In other words, black people do not merely interface with police departments as suspects and offenders, but also as crime victims, lawyers, witnesses, public defenders, social workers, judges, corrections officers, probation officers, beat cops, city administrators, and wardens, especially in cities like Baltimore, Washington, DC, Chicago, and others with sizable black populations. White's defense of black sentiment, against my critique, forces these differences out of view, and gives the impression that all blacks, "we," view the problems of crime and punishment in the same ways, and are ready to prioritize the same raft of solutions. In fact, she concludes, "the well-being of Blacks always also requires—as a means to attend to accumulating, historical, unfair disadvantage—a collective sense of Black self-determination." This view that the black population constitutes a cohesive political constituency with commonly held interests was not true during the Jim Crow era, and it is certainly not a useful way of thinking about black political life now.

Black life was complex under Jim Crow segregation, albeit cramped by de jure and social constraints imposed on black political will in the North and South. Black political life was and is animated by competing interests and different visions of what society should be. Such dynamics took on a unique character in different epochs given the broad experience of slavery and Jim Crow segregation, but the fact of noncitizen or second-class-citizenship status did not generate a unified set of aspirations and interests among blacks, even if some projected the sense of common black passions and strivings to suit their particular interests as black leaders (or scholars), white benefactors, or white supremacists.

The black population has experienced profound demographic and political changes since the fifties. Poverty has decreased since the landmark 1954 *Brown v. Board of Education* decision, which overturned the "separate but equal" precedent on which the Jim Crow edifice stood, from the plight of the vast majority of blacks to the experience of roughly a quarter of the black population. The black middle class expanded after World War II, and black integration into mass culture as consumers and producers, and in higher education, employment, corporations, the nonprofit world, and public sector employment, was spurred by omnibus civil rights legislation as well as opportunities provided by New Deal, Fair Deal, and Great Society programs. In many locales, black governance became a reality. By the late 1980s, the three largest American cities elected black mayors, and by then, the presence of black mayors and black city council majorities were the norm wherever there was a sizable black electorate. These changes were the consequence of popular pressure and the public policy it produced, the initiatives of the New Deal Democratic coalition and the Johnson White House.

Somehow, in our contemporary moment, the New Deal coalition has been recast as the villains of history. However, that narrative, now orthodox among many on the left, silences the actually existing historical voices and experiences of blacks who benefited from, supported, and fought to expand the policies of the New Deal, Fair Deal, and Great Society periods. Even worse still, this narrative breeds cynicism, leaving us with a wrongheaded view of the political process, and what the left might do now, under very different social and political conditions, to abolish poverty; decommodify housing, health care, transportation, education, and other basic needs; and expand popular democratic power within the economic realm—all of which, like the eradication of police brutality, would disproportionately, though not solely, benefit black citizens. It does not take much thought to conclude that the form of social democracy produced by the New Deal coalition was limited, especially compared to other industrialized nations, but it takes a particular type of bad faith to conclude that the horizon of contemporary left aspirations should be limited by the history of the New Deal.

The sheer size of the black population today should in and of itself render such talk of "black self-organization" and "black sentiment" obsolete. At nearly 46 million, the black population in the United States is greater than the population of Canada, three times the size of the population of Greece, and slightly larger than the combined population of Oceania (i.e., Australasia, Melanesia, Polynesia, and Micronesia). Why are so many incapable of thinking about the black population with the same complexity they would afford those populations? To his credit, Moody does briefly acknowledge the fact of different class interests among blacks, but he does not provide the kind of historical materialist analysis that you might expect from someone who has dedicated most of his adult life to the study of class struggle. Despite his posturing about the "right to black self-organization," it is interesting that when Moody encounters such self-activity in all its contradictory, historical motion, he has difficulty realizing its import. Rather than a full-bodied class analysis of black political life, his claims instead resemble the more familiar culturalist arguments of class from the Black Power lectern. In other words, all the black elites are either dupes or sellouts, the black working class and poor are victims, and somewhere, lurking around the historical corner, is the revolutionary black subject waiting to be born.

Moody recognizes the "contradictory and even reactionary role" of black elites in shaping punishment policy, only to shrug off their influence, concluding they played "most certainly a subordinate role in terms of federal and state policy and practice." Here Moody mischaracterizes the actual dynamics of the carceral buildup, a process that took place largely at the local and state level, the very contexts where black political power and mobilization mattered. The role of black public officials within the contexts of cities like Washington, DC, Detroit, New Orleans, and elsewhere was anything but subordinate. Subordinate to whom? Moody misses the very powerful role that these black elites played and continue to play in formal party politics and local economic growth regimes, in legitimating neoliberalization and, at times, insulating such forces from criticism even when they embark on policy decisions that will have negative social consequences for black constituencies.

More troubling, Moody diminishes the role that various black constituencies, neighborhood groups, landlords, business owners, clergy, educators, and activists, not simply political elites, played in shaping the carceral expansion. The sense of different subject positions among blacks, which cannot be reduced simply to the "petty bourgeoisie" and the "long struggle for black freedom" as Moody does, is totally lost. Moody refers to the demands of working-class blacks for more police protection and tougher crime policy, but in a manner that returns quickly to the victim narrative, disconnecting their conscious actions as citizens from their unintended consequence, mass incarceration. James Forman Jr.,

Michael Javen Fortner, and Donna Murch among others have provided a more useful sense of how these processes unfolded in real time and space, and the different motives that animated distinct black political choices.[4]

There were liberal and progressive blacks and whites in Washington, DC, who supported decriminalization of marijuana and a handgun ban, and black nationalist community activists who opposed both measures. We would never know these details if we were to adhere to Moody's generalizations about black life. More importantly, black opposition to both of those measures, policies which most urban dwellers would champion as progressive today, actually mattered. The legislation was defeated, marijuana arrests over the next few decades contributed mightily to the carceral expansion, and the proliferation of handguns made the District of Columbia one of the most dangerous cities in the United States.

As my comrade Adolph Reed Jr. has cautioned, "Taxonomy is not critique." Merely addressing the alleged excesses and missteps of black elites, without much concern for what class means in daily lives, organizational contexts, and real political fights, cannot stand in for serious analysis of how black life is organized in myriad ways, like that of all other Americans, by the processes of production and realization of surplus value. A first basic step in a critical-left analysis is acknowledging the actual forces at play within black political life, rather than falling back on Black Power rhetorical formulas. These problems in Moody's essay come into even sharper relief when he attempts to defend the liberal racial justice frame.

Policing Surplus Population

> This is my eleventh year of being shoveled into every major prison in the most populous state in the nation, and the largest prison system in the world . . . Hidden are the facts that, at each institution I've been in, 30 to sometimes 40 percent of those held are black, and *every one* of the many thousands I've encountered was from the working or lumpenproletariat class.
>
> —George Jackson, *Blood in My Eye* (1972)

The argument that contemporary policing in the United States is fundamentally about managing relative surplus population has been advanced by neo-Marxist and socialist thinkers over the last fifty years, from George Jackson's prison writings to Stuart Hall et al.'s *Policing the Crisis* and Ruth Wilson Gilmore's *Golden Gulag*, among others.[5] Although they do not employ a Marxist analytical framework, other critical social scientists have drawn similar conclusions regarding the class character of mass incarceration. Loïc Wacquant's notions of the hyperghetto and hyperincarceration focus on submerged segments of the black urban population who are most heavily targeted by police and most likely to be incarcerated.[6] In a similar vein, Brett Story critically engages the concept of the "million-dollar block," which denotes the spatially concentrated origins of the nation's 2.3 million prisoners in a handful of dense urban neighborhoods that are the target of massive state investments in policing and incarceration.[7] All of the aforementioned works acknowledge very visible racial inequalities, and begin from a basic sense of racial justice as a cherished political value. What they also share, however, is a more discerning interpretation of which portions of the black population have borne the brunt of the carceral expansion, and what those segments share with similarly situated prisoners, parolees, and ex-offenders across ethnic and racial groups.

Thinking about mass incarceration in terms of surplus population helps us to name precisely those who are most regularly surveilled and harassed by police, and who are the most likely to have their livelihoods as ex-offenders determined by the long reach of the carceral state. Unlike the New Jim Crow framing, discussing relative surplus population focuses our attention on which portions of the black population are most likely to be subject to intensive surveillance and policing. Although many blacks experience racial profiling in policing practices and in retail consumer contexts, class is a much more powerful determinant of who is actually arrested, assigned a public defender, convicted, sentenced, and incarcerated.

Moody notes that the carceral state is "very selective of which white people are most likely to be arrested, tried and incarcerated." These same selective dynamics, however, are at play across other US populations, including African Americans. Blacks are disproportionately represented among those who are arrested, convicted, incarcerated, and under court supervision because blacks are still disproportionately represented among the nation's poor. Hence, if poor neighborhoods and communities are over-policed, then it is no wonder, as Moody notes, that "blacks are almost six times and

Latinos three times more likely to be sentenced to 'hard time' in prison than whites."

I have never denied these racial disparities, but what I have argued instead is that these racial disparities regarding policing and incarceration mirror the demography of the most vulnerable segments of the working class. Moody pins the disproportionate sentencing of blacks and Latinos to prison time compared to whites on discrimination, but without much consideration of other underlying dynamics. Namely, he neglects how poverty and the compulsory use of underfunded and overextended public defender's offices produce the kinds of disproportionality in conviction rates across race. What appears as racial disparity is, underneath it all, a function of class power and dispossession. By focusing on the broader problem of relative surplus population, we might well connect these discussions of mass incarceration to the broader problems of capitalist society, as well as make common cause with the millions of over-policed Americans who do not fit into a Black Lives Matter framework. In other words, the problem of mass incarceration as we know it is not an aberration, but rather a constitutive part of governing in the aftermath of welfare state liberalism.

In an odd interpretative move for a veteran labor historian, Moody seizes on employment status at the time of arrest, as though that moment tells us all we need to know about the lives of this segment of the working class. Moody offers a rather selective reading of incarceration statistics, one guided by an understanding of class that seems closer to behavioralist social science than historical materialism. He contends that those who are sentenced to prison are not primarily drawn from the surplus population. To evidence this point he refers to a study by the National Center for Education Statistics, although the full citation for this study is not provided. Moody reports "nearly two-thirds of the prison population were employed prior to incarceration. Forty-nine percent of all prisoners were employed full-time and another 16 percent in part-time work before entering prison, while another 8 percent were students, retired, or permanently disabled." Moody then notes "only 19 percent of prisoners in 2014 were unemployed at the time of incarceration."

The statistics that Moody attributes to the National Center for Education Statistics were drawn from a 2014 survey conducted by the Program for International Assessment of Adult Competencies, a research initiative of the Organisation for Economic Co-operation and Development that assesses literacy and skill levels for workforce development. That survey was taken between February and June 2014 and included 1,315 inmates—1,048 males and 267 females. I am not sure why Moody chose this data when there are other sources that provide decidedly fuller and more rigorous portraits of the pre-arrest experiences of those who are incarcerated.[8] I am also not as confident as Moody that we can make useful generalizations from this sample, one that was drawn from a selection of prisons. This is especially a concern regarding any conclusions about women, who constitute a fast-growing incarcerated population. Most importantly, we should not make historical generalizations about carceral dynamics that have taken shape slowly and unevenly across the country over the last half century based on one year's worth of data, no matter how fulsome it might be. Like so much analysis in this vein, complexity and context, be it within black political life or in the differing policies of states ranging from Louisiana to Minnesota, seem to fall away in favor of easy moralism. Still, there are bigger interpretive problems here with both this particular use of employment statistics to discuss class, and his sense of the argument we have made regarding relative surplus population and policing.

As Moody well knows, class is not merely a matter of employment or income but rather is more fundamentally about the social relations of production. The relative surplus population, or "reserve army" as Marx developed the concept, cannot be reduced to latter-day metrics of unemployment. Class is set in historical motion, and the reserve army represents a relative, contingent condition of the working class, rather than an ascriptive status. Marx denoted four fluid layers of the reserve army: a *floating* reserve of the temporarily employed; a *latent* segment made up of those not actively looking for work, but who may be mobilized to meet capital's shifting valorization requirements; a *stagnant* portion of those with "extremely irregular" employment; and lastly, the sphere of *pauperism*, which is the "hospital of active labor-army and the dead weight of the industrial reserve army."[9] These populations are not fixed; rather, their composition is expanding and contracting relative to the dictates of capital's need for living labor.

Employment status at the time of arrest is only part of the story in the lives of those governed through incarceration.

For too many, it is after their sentence has been served that the real work of management of surplus population begins. The prospects of gainful employment for ex-offenders are greatly diminished by the combined force of the social stigma and discrimination they face, mandatory conviction self-reporting on job and college admissions applications, and the denial of access to public relief, unemployment insurance, and housing assistance in some states.[10]

Ex-offenders are also compelled to take low-wage work to meet the requirements of and avoid punishment under an elaborate, manipulative probation system.[11] In their empirically rich study of the ex-offender employability crisis, Jamie Peck and Nik Theodore focused on Chicago's majority black, West Side neighborhoods of North Lawndale, East and West Garfield Park, and Austin, which are home to the highest concentrations of returning ex-offenders in the nation. They conclude that upon returning home to Chicago, ex-offenders face a "profoundly inhospitable labor market." Moreover, Peck and Theodore contend that "the prison system has become a labor market institution of considerable significance . . . configuring prevailing definitions of employability, shaping the social distribution of work and wages, prefiguring the terms under which different segments of the contingent labor supply enter the job market, and shaping their relative bargaining power."[12]

A growing swell of policy activism has been dedicated to toppling these barriers to economic mobility facing formerly incarcerated persons. Such political efforts have borne some fruit in recent years, with many states passing "ban the box" legislation, ending mandatory self-reporting of prior convictions on job applications and college admissions, but critics rightly argue these policies do not go far enough to eliminate discrimination against ex-offenders. The fact remains that the carceral state contributes greatly to the reproduction of the industrial reserve, and in a manner that is intimately connected to the postindustrial urban economies.

Moody lifts my discussion of policing surplus population out of the context of the gentrifying city, missing the ways that aggressive policing is central to urban real estate development and tourism-entertainment sector growth, both of which serve as central economic drivers in the contemporary landscape. Moody seems to forget that since the late eighties and the accelerated, broad adoption of zero tolerance strategies, the overwhelming resources of contemporary policing are dedicated to the routine surveillance, targeting, arrest, and prosecution of those whose activities are a means of basic survival and who are only nominally or infrequently employed in the formal wage economy. Much of routine policing activity is focused on regulating criminalized forms of work—panhandling, busking, sex work, the drug trade, property crime, operating as an unlicensed vendor, the illegal trade in stolen merchandise, and, to be frank, robbery and mugging, keeping in mind that slightly more than half of the incarcerated were convicted of violent offenses. There is also ample evidence that such deployments of more aggressive policing tactics are meted out in explicitly segregative ways that maintain the class order, insuring perpetual accumulation, on one hand, by defending middle-class and affluent consumer spaces, tourism districts, office parks, and gentrifying neighborhoods, and on the other, by regulating the poor, homeless, so-called "disconnected youth," noncitizen workers, and criminalized forms of work.[13]

Finally, Moody's defense of the New Jim Crow sensibility neglects recent and well-publicized trends in carceral demography, changes that further erode the claim that the carceral expansion of the last four decades was primarily driven by racial disparity in anti-drug policy. Between 2000 and 2015, the black male incarceration rate fell by more than 24 percent, while rates for white men climbed slightly. During the same period, the incarceration rate for black women declined by nearly 50 percent, while the inverse was true for white women, who experienced a 53 percent increase.[14]

This is progress on the racial justice front, perhaps a consequence of the sharpening public debate and intensity of local and state-level organizing. Yet at the same time, such changes are a reminder that the carceral state's underlying motives are not fully captured in slogans like the "New Jim Crow" or "Black Lives Matter." A dogged fixation on racial disparities only provides a narrow window on the carceral crisis. That is a window that we are familiar with; it connects rather easily to liberal interpretations of American society and organizing strategies that survived the Cold War, while other modes of working-class analysis and social action were criminalized and eviscerated. Shifting our attention to the problem of relative surplus population allows us to see the connections between the plight of black teenagers from Chicago's "wild hundreds," arrested for their part in a "flash mob" robbery of a Magnificent Mile clothing store, and that of a white middle-aged mother, her son, and his live-in girlfriend who are arrested for selling OxyContin in their small town in southern Missouri. Marxist analyses of mass incarceration should be able to account for such situated experiences of the working class in the post-Fordist economy.

Mythologizing the New Deal

White and Moody advance and enlarge popular fictions about New Deal social democracy and its racial limitations that have become new orthodoxies on the American left. And true to form, their attempts to root out the limitations of the New Deal silence black citizens' historical responses to New Deal policy, reflected in part by the large-scale migration of black voters into the Democratic Party ranks from the Depression onward. "The benefits of universal programs such as the New Deal," White declares, "cannot be misremembered as materially transforming for the better the lives of the most marginalized Black Americans."

White contends, "The New Deal is widely critiqued for failing Black people, specifically because most New Deal Programs discriminated against Blacks, authorized separate and lower pay scales for Blacks, refused outright to support Black Applicants (for example, the Federal Housing Authority refused to guarantee mortgages for Blacks who tried to buy in white neighborhoods), and the Civilian Conservation Corps maintained segregated camps." She then turns to the familiar claim that the farm and domestic worker exemptions of the

1935 Social Security Act are irrefutable evidence of the racist limitations of the New Deal policy legacy.[15] This is a falsehood repeated so many times that it is now widely accepted as true.

Southern Democrats certainly sought to exclude black workers from protections, as historian Touré Reed argues; however, "the most obvious problem with the claim is that it ignores the fact that the majority of sharecroppers, tenant farmers, mixed farm laborers and domestic workers in the early 1930s were white." Some 11.4 million whites were employed as agricultural laborers and domestics, compared to 3.5 million blacks. As such, Reed reminds us, the Social Security exemptions excluded 27 percent of all white workers nationally.[16] As a historical explanation of the New Deal's limitations, the *Jim Crow–ing* of national social policy thesis does not hold up, nor is it based in the preponderance of actual research by historians themselves. Rather, the power of particular capitalist blocs prevailed, in this case the landed interests represented by the Farm Bureau, insuring the vulnerability of the most submerged and dispossessed workers.

This New Deal mythology also wipes clean the record of black support and influence over the subsequent trajectory of Roosevelt-era reforms, and those pursued after the Second World War. There is little mention in their account of the massive public works programs that employed thousands of blacks, namely the Civilian Conservation Corps (CCC) or the Works Progress Administration (WPA).[17] These public works projects were publicly funded and publicly managed, employing millions of Americans from all walks of life. The CCC workers built roads and bridges, refurbished portions of the Appalachian Trail, and developed numerous public amenities of the US parks service.

There was no doubt discrimination in the CCC program. Black enrollment was capped at 10 percent of total enrollment, which mirrored the black proportion of the national population. As Nick Taylor points out, this level of CCC employment did not meet the high demand for relief among African Americans who were especially hard hit by the Depression.[18] White nevertheless overreaches in claiming that all CCCs were segregated. In the Deep South CCC camps were segregated, sadly in conformity with the Jim Crow order, but beyond the Mason-Dixon line, many CCC work camps were integrated. All told, between 1933 and 1941, some 250,000 blacks were enrolled in the corps.

Luther Wandall summed up his experience in the CCC this way in the pages of *Crisis* Magazine: "On the whole, I was gratified rather than disappointed with the CCC. I had expected the worst. Of course, it reflects, to some extent, all the practices and prejudices of the U.S. Army. But as a job and an experience, for a man who has no work, I can heartily recommend it."[19] Wandall's comments, which are unsentimental and critical, and the scores of similar testimonies by other black men and boys who joined the CCC camps, should caution us against interpreting the meaning of New Deal social policies for its historical constituencies against the din of contemporary debates and preoccupations. There is a parallel dissonance between the actual experience of the GI

Bill's educational and training provisions by black service-men nationally, and contemporary efforts to impugn the policy as evidence of meta-historical white supremacy.[20]

In the case of the WPA, it undertook a range of projects that provided work and income to millions of Americans, who were employed in the construction of public buildings, public art, music and theater projects, literacy programs, and the development of tourist guides for every state in the union. In 1935, blacks constituted around 15 percent of the WPA workforce, some 350,000, at least in raw numbers dispropor-tionately benefiting from the program vis-à-vis whites. Ironically enough, many black writers who are now canon-ized by contemporary anti-racist liberals—writers like Dorothy West, Richard Wright, Margaret Walker, and Zora Neale Hurston, to name a few—were employed through the Federal Writers' Project. Likewise, one significant but forgot-ten achievement of the WPA was the oral history project undertaken by John Lomax and Sterling Brown that collected the stories of hundreds of antebellum slavery's survivors, by then in their eighties and nineties, providing us with a price-less audio archive of their perspectives on bondage and free-dom. These clearly anti-racist dimensions of the New Deal are buried underneath convenient and often errant readings of the motives behind certain policies, their implications for black citizens, and the actual responses from black publics who lived and worked in the context.

It should be noted, as well, that thousands of black work-ers were unionized in the steel mills, automotive plants, pack-inghouses, and ports across the United States during the

Depression, World War II, and after because of the right to collective bargaining under the Wagner Act.[21] The wages they earned in these industries, and in many cases their unions themselves, became the key economic bulwark of the later civil rights movement.

More evidence of the complex relationship between black popular struggles and the Roosevelt administration can be seen in the passage of Executive Order 8802. This measure desegregated the defense industries, drawing thousands of blacks into the wartime workforce, and was signed under the threat of a national protest—the original "March on Washington Movement" organized by black trade unionist A. Philip Randolph.[22]

In attempting to characterize it as a type of "identity politics," Moody misreads the context of Randolph's leadership of the original March on Washington Movement. Moody contends that Randolph and Rustin were committed to black self-organization, but this is a rather superficial and anachronistic reading of the historical moment and the choices Randolph made in his attempt to desegregate the defense industries. Moody refers to Randolph rather dismissively as a "self-proclaimed socialist" before claiming that the planned March on Washington, and later formations such as the Negro American Labor Council, represent commitments to "identity politics" before the term came into existence. "Was this 'identity politics' without the label?" Moody asks, "Or was it the recognition that in the struggle for black freedom and equality, black self-organization was an indispensable tool, even (or perhaps particularly) where unity and solidarity with whites was (as in the labor movement) expected but often denied?"

The simple answer is no, it was not identity politics. Randolph was clear in his opposition to the most nationalistic styles of politics among blacks, as evidenced in his vocal support for the "Garvey Must Go" campaign. Moody's reliance on the white New Left and more contemporary radical fetish of black self-organization also gets in the way of useful interpretation of this moment. Of course, Randolph demanded full black participation, and crisscrossed the nation to stoke black citizen commitments, precisely because the black population was an expanding bloc of the Democratic Party coalition. It was the New Deal, after all, that began the process of black exodus from the party of Lincoln. Somehow, Moody glosses this important fact of national political context and why it would be important for Randolph and his allies to prepare for a strong show of force of the emerging black electorate. For the record, whether the left should acknowledge black self-organization or not is someone else's battle—one with origins in the white New Left's nearly pathological search for political relevancy and authentic revolutionary subjecthood as they stood uneasily between concomitant black political struggles in the fifties and sixties, and the growing social conservatism that accompanied the expansion of the mostly white, suburban middle class.

Public works projects, black workers' participation in union struggles, and the desegregation of the defense industries altered public perceptions about race and gender equality, brought Americans from different backgrounds into real and often unprecedented contact with one another, and presaged the expansion and new assertiveness of civil rights campaigns after the war. These reforms also meant real, tangible improvements in the lives of millions of African Americans and so frequently provided the material context in which they could more easily participate in civil rights struggles. Rather than seeing the era of New Deal reform as a great exception, and as yet another episode where American politics is hemmed in by the "original sin" of race, we should situate the era more firmly within domestic and international class struggle, the historic effort of the US capitalist class to save the system from its own contradictions amid the Depression, and the countervailing movement of popular and labor forces to impose a more just order.[23] This was exceptional in the sense that it marked a period when capital was forced to take responsibility for the costs of social reproduction of labor, a function it has abandoned, with far-reaching and disruptive social consequences, under decades of neoliberalization, the dismantling of the welfare state apparatus, and the privatization of formerly public goods and services.

As they have migrated from the scholarly studies of Ira Katznelson, Jefferson Cowie, and others to the popular renditions of Ta-Nehisi Coates, and into the realm of left common sense, the "New Deal was racist" narrative has often conflated the Depression-era New Deal policies with work of the New Deal Democratic coalition after the Second World War. In the process, such accounts run together and roundly condemn policies that were produced through distinct geopolitical contexts, characterized by a shifting balance of class forces, changing partisan and congressional leadership, and different strategic logics.

The first and second New Deal enacted under Franklin D. Roosevelt reflected the growing power of organized labor, and concessions made by capital for the assurance of continued social stability and uninterrupted compound growth. The Fair Deal enacted after the war under the leadership of Harry Truman set in a motion a commercial Keynesian transformation of urban society through the 1949 Housing Act. The expansion of federally backed mortgage lending, massive investments in urban renewal, and inner-city public housing construction shifted away from the state-funded and state-managed public works of the Depression, creating a bonanza for real estate capital, local construction trades, architectural firms, and manufacturers of industrial building materials. If there is a policy initiative of the New Deal coalition that should be roundly condemned, it is this 1949 measure that entrenched racial and class inequalities into a new metropolitan spatial order. The sixties saw efforts of New Deal Democrats to rectify these inequalities, again an important historical detail that is obliterated in the sweeping brushstrokes of the "constraint of race" narrative. The result was a wave of national anti-racist and anti-poverty legislation that produced major social progress, but inasmuch as Great Society legislation avoided direct, aggressive market interventions, such measures failed to create the same structures of employment for the black urban poor that had been produced over time for many whites through public works, defense contracting and industrialization, and the right to collective bargaining.[24]

Why Rustin Still Matters

Both White and Moody attempt to cast doubt on the prospects of universal public policy in our times. They both abide the "constraint of race" thesis, that is that any and all attempts to create social policy that might benefit the greatest number of Americans will ultimately fail because of racism, or in a slightly different iteration, that universal public policies will only retrench existing racial disparities of wealth, income, health care, housing, and education.

Moody concludes that my politics are afflicted by nostalgia for the realignment theory touted by Rustin and Michael Harrington. Mind you, he extrapolates this claim from a passing reference to Rustin in my 2017 *Catalyst* essay, where I briefly criticize Rustin's turn to "politics of insider negotiation" before touting the merits of the 1966 *Freedom Budget* he co-authored with Randolph, and lamenting its being eclipsed by Cold War liberals' rather narrow focus on institutional racism and the alleged cultural pathologies of the poor. Somehow, Moody interprets my embrace of that agenda with a wholesale acceptance of Rustin's increasingly conservative commitments to the Democratic Party. In the process, he misreads both Rustin's politics and mine.

I have criticized Rustin's conservative turn in various places, characterizing him as a tragic figure in my 2007 book *Revolutionaries to Race Leaders*, and that argument largely channeled sociologist Stephen Steinberg's analysis that appeared in *New Politics* a decade earlier.[25] Moody doesn't attempt to contextualize and explain Rustin's increasing conservatism, so I will here. It is no secret now that Rustin was a marginalized figure during the early stages of the postwar civil rights movement; he was forced to play an offstage role, serving as a mentor to Martin Luther King Jr. and a key strategist in various demonstrations that would prove pivotal to the growing movement to topple Jim Crow. He was held at bay by clergy because of his gay sexuality and youthful communist commitments, which made him an easy target for segregationists, the FBI, and other foes of racial progress looking to derail the Southern campaigns. After having been closeted within the leadership circles of the postwar movement for years, Rustin finally found himself taking on a more public role as broker between the movement and the Kennedy White House. He justifies his choice of insider negotiation over popular protests in his 1965 *Commentary* essay, but in the process Rustin wrongly confines popular struggles to an expired stage in black political development.[26]

Rustin's problem was twofold. He simply misread his times, and perhaps more fatally, he jettisoned mass mobilization and civil disobedience, which had been fundamental to the postwar civil rights movement, in favor of brokerage politics with the Democratic Party. He thought the passage of major civil rights legislation was the beginning of a new political stage, one that would make it possible to push for deeper, broader social reforms exclusively through the formal democratic process. As I said in 2015, in an extended interview with University of Illinois-Chicago graduate student Gregor Baszak,

> I doubt Rustin's wisdom at that historical moment. His belief that participation sans protest could steer the Democratic Party during the middle '60s towards more extensive commitments to social democracy seems even more foolhardy in hindsight. He had reason to be optimistic about the prospects given the Johnson administration's civil rights reforms and the War on Poverty, but there were very real reactionary tendencies within the Democratic Party at that time. The party included Vietnam hawks, Southern segregationists, and legions of voters who were firmly committed to the middle-class consumer society. Rustin cedes too much ground to them. And, again, his fatal flaw is that he no longer seems to appreciate the role of movement pressure.[27]

Hence, Rustin surrendered the repertoire of movement strategies that might have enabled African Americans and other more progressive elements in American society to press for more substantial policy reforms, such as those contained in the 1966 *Freedom Budget*.

Despite his strategic missteps and rightward drift, Rustin's criticisms of black separatism and Black Power militancy remain relevant in this tide of Black Lives Matter. His claim, cited by Moody, that the "future of the Negro struggle depends on whether the contradictions of this society can be resolved by a coalition of progressive forces which becomes the effective political majority in the United States" remains powerful, and unfulfilled. Rustin was clear, and we should be as well, that every major political advance of blacks in US history was not merely the outcome of "self-organization" of the oppressed, but rather the result of a diverse cast of political actors. The abolition of slavery, the short-lived advances of federal Reconstruction, the discrete gains of blacks during the Roosevelt administration, and the toppling of the Jim Crow system were achieved through the self-activity of some blacks, the principled commitment of nonblacks to historically concrete forms of social justice, and the begrudging acceptance of still others that the status quo, whether slavery or Jim Crow, was no longer sustainable.

In slightly different ways, White and Moody both characterize me as some sort of Democratic loyalist who sees the future of blacks or the laboring classes more generally in closing ranks with the Democratic Party. In an odd conclusion, Moody claims that the Sanders wave and surging interest in class analysis and socialism, especially among millennials, may in fact lead to a mass migration of the left into the Democratic Party ranks. "With this renewed hope," Moody writes, "has come a demotion of race as a subject of socioeconomic analysis in the name of class that is, in reality, a return to America's quintessential business-funded, neoliberal-dominated, undemocratic, cross-class social construction: the Democratic Party." White reaches a similar conclusion, "whereas the pivot to support class political interests along party lines with the kind of power and influence Johnson seeks has not demonstrated to Black Americans the kind of mutuality and support required in an ongoing, historically and cumulatively race-class reality." They both fear that emphasizing a class-conscious politics, and organizing around commonly felt needs—that is, those basic necessities that we all require for reproduction, such as food, clothing, housing that is safe and appropriate to our specific needs and life stage, health care, education, time, and space for creative expression and recreation—will consolidate power among the Democrats, and likely produce policies that retrench racial inequalities. I could not disagree more with their conclusions in this regard.

What should be clear to anyone paying attention is that the New Democrats are much more willing to embrace versions of liberal anti-racism than they are willing to make substantial commitments to broadly redistributive public policy. The Bill Clinton administration pioneered this combination of socially liberal public relations and pro-capitalist national economic and social policy, which included workfare reform and the demolition of public housing via HOPE VI legislation. The Obama administration perfected this combination of socially liberal public relations and neoliberal governance, drawing on his claims to racial authenticity to deflect public criticism and popular outrage over black employment and police killings. The field of 2020 Democratic presidential hopefuls features more of the same, with some like Cory Booker, Elizabeth Warren, and Kamala Harris already floating their version of black reparations, in concert with a growing list of neoliberal reparations devotees, including *Forbes* magazine contributors and *New York Times* columnist David

Brooks.[28] Far from opposing a politics of recognition and racial justice, Democratic centrists are in full embrace of underrepresented minorities, as evidenced in triumphant public and partisan interpretations of the 2018 midterm elections. Equally, they are committed to addressing wealth inequality so long as the proposed policies do not disrupt the sanctity of private property. Put another way, the New Democrats are prepared to do what they have done for the last few decades: continue their low-frequency war against the working class, while embracing racial and gender justice for those who are the most integrated and ideologically committed to neoliberalism.

The only way I think we can reverse this process, and contest the power of capital, which is enshrined in both parties, is to build working class–centered popular struggles and fight to achieve universal, concrete forms of social justice that improve the lives of the greatest number of Americans. Unlike these authors, I believe that politics and context matters, that addressing the expressed needs and desires of working-class Americans need not forever be haunted by the alleged and real failings of the New Deal, Fair Deal, or Great Society regimes of national policy-making.

This is an ahistorical point that I wish so many on the left would stop making. It is wrong in terms of historical analysis and politically defeatist as an operating logic. We know that universal policies like Social Security and the national public works programs of the Depression era made life better for millions of Americans. We also know that national anti-discrimination regulation improved the lives of African

Americans, expanding the middle class, reducing poverty, and integrating blacks more fully into American life. The lives of millions more could be improved through a combination of universal policies that decommodify housing, education, health care, and transportation; effective anti-discrimination laws that prohibit racist behavior in housing, job markets, and higher education admissions; and federal, state, and local policies that address inequalities in K–12 school district funding, and that strengthen the right to collective bargaining and raise wage floors.

As I and others have argued before, broad swaths of the black population have long supported universal, progressive social policies, often with greater intensity than other segments of the US population. Although we recall the sixties as a heyday of black "self-organization" and the reactionary unionism of George Meany, African Americans were the most likely to join a union during that period. We need a left analysis of American history and contemporary life that proceeds from a clearheaded sense of actually existing black life. We should not shy away from pursuing these policies because of perceived historical failures, or worse, because of some paranoia of co-optation by the Democratic Party. Both of those concerns seem academic in the worst way to me, divorced from the daily realities and tough choices that many Americans are forced to make at the ballot box and on payday. The nominal left is already an adjunct to the Democratic Party, largely because of prevalent antipathy among remnants of Occupy Wall Street and Black Lives Matter toward consti-tuted power, and the real difficulty of building popular power in the pro-capitalist and anti-public environment that neoliberalization has produced. In places where the infrastructure and organizing networks exists, socialists should run for public office and build an independent political base, but this is not possible in some parts of the country.

We need a left politics that organizes for power, and draws a keen distinction between supporting Democratic candidates in specific locales where they are a better option, and building a left politics that cannot be subsumed under the Democratic Party and is ultimately capable of emancipating labor and empowering the masses of Americans. Rustin's basic majoritarian claim, that the left can only win—and implicitly that African Americans can only win—by building powerful alliances capable of imposing popular will and contesting the demands capital makes on the planet and our lives, remains very much in front of us.

Notes

Preface: The Triumph of Black Lives
Matter and Neoliberal Redemption

1. Adolph Reed Jr., "How Racial Disparity Does Not Help Make Sense of Patterns of Police Violence," *Nonsite*, September 16, 2016, nonsite.org.
2. "Protesters' Anger Justified, Even If Actions May Not Be," Monmouth University Polling Institute, June 2, 2020, monmouth.edu/polling-institute/reports/monmouthpoll_us_060220.

Introduction

1. See, inter alia, Thomas F. Jackson, *From Civil Rights to Human Rights: Martin Luther King Jr. and the Struggle for Economic Justice* (Philadelphia: University of Pennsylvania Press, 2007); Sylvie Laurent, *King and the Other America: The Poor People's Campaign and the Quest for Economic Security* (Berkeley: University of California Press, 2018); William P. Jones, *The March on Washington: Jobs, Freedom and the Forgotten History of Civil Rights* (New York: W.W. Norton, 2013); Michael K. Honey, *To the Promised Land: Martin Luther King and the Fight for Economic Justice* (New York: W.W. Norton, 2018).
2. See Bayard Rustin, *Strategies for Freedom: The Changing Patterns of Black Protest* (New York: Columbia University Press, 1976), esp. Chapter 3, 56–78.

3. See Cedric Johnson, *Revolutionaries to Race Leaders: Black Power and the Making of African American Politics* (Minneapolis: University of Minnesota Press, 2007).

1 The Panthers Can't Save Us Now

1. Alicia Garza, "A Herstory of the #BlackLivesMatter Movement," *Feminist Wire*, October 7, 2014, thefeministwire.com.

2. Arnold R. Hirsch, *Making the Second Ghetto: Race and Housing in Chicago, 1940–1960* (Chicago: University of Chicago Press, 1998); Preston H. Smith II, *Racial Democracy in the Black Metropolis: Housing Policy in Postwar Chicago* (Minneapolis: University of Minnesota, 2012); Beryl Satter, *Family Properties: How the Struggle over Race and Real Estate Transformed Chicago and Urban America* (New York: Metropolitan Books, 2009); N.D.B. Connolly, *A World More Concrete: Real Estate and the Making of Jim Crow South Florida* (Chicago: University of Chicago Press, 2014).

3. James Boggs, *The American Revolution: Pages from a Negro Worker's Notebook* (New York: Monthly Review, 1963).

4. Lyndon B. Johnson, "Commencement Address at Howard University: 'To Fulfill These Rights,' " June 4, 1965.

5. See Michael Harrington, *The Other America: Poverty in the United States* (New York: Macmillan, 1962); Kenneth Clark, *Dark Ghetto: Dilemmas of Social Power* (New York: Harper & Row, 1965).

6. Rhonda Levine, *Class Struggle and the New Deal: Industrial Labor, Industrial Capital and the State* (Lawrence: University Press of Kansas, 1988).

7. Nelson Lichtenstein, *State of the Union: A Century of American Labor* (Princeton, NJ: Princeton University Press, 2002), 114–20.

8. Touré F. Reed, "Why Liberals Separate Race from Class," *Jacobin*, August 22, 2015; Touré F. Reed, "Why Moynihan Was Not so Misunderstood at the Time: The Mythological Prescience of the Moynihan Report and the Problem of Institutional Structuralism," *Nonsite* 17, September 4, 2015; William P. Jones, *The March on Washington: Jobs, Freedom and the Forgotten History of Civil Rights* (New York: W.W. Norton, 2013).

9. Bayard Rustin, " 'Black Power' and Coalition Politics," *Commentary*, September 1966, 35–40; Bayard Rustin, "The Failure of Black Separatism," *Harper's*, January 1970.

10. A. Philip Randolph and Bayard Rustin, *A Freedom Budget for All Americans: A Summary* (New York: A. Philip Randolph Institute, 1967).

11. Kent B. Germany, *New Orleans after the Promises: Poverty, Citizenship and the Search for the Great Society* (Atlanta: University of Georgia Press, 2007), 15–16.

12. Daniel Patrick Moynihan, *Maximum Feasible Misunderstanding: Community Action in the War on Poverty* (New York: Free Press, 1970).

13. Harold Cruse, *The Crisis of the Negro Intellectual* (New York: William Morrow, 1967); Stokely Carmichael and Charles V. Hamilton, *Black Power: The Politics of Liberation in America* (New York: Vintage, 1967).

14. Ibid., 9–10.

15. Carmichael and Hamilton, *Black Power*, 44–45.

16. Cedric Johnson, "Panther Nostalgia as History," *New Labor Forum* 23, no. 2 (May 2014), 112–15.

17. Robert Allen, *Black Awakening in Capitalist America: An Analytic History* (New York: Anchor Books, 1969), 18–19.

18. Ibid.

19. Adolph Reed Jr., "Black Urban Regime: Structural Origins and Constraints," in *Stirrings in the Jug: Black Politics in the Postsegregation Era* (Minneapolis: University of Minnesota Press, 1999), 97.

20. Movement for Black Lives, *Vision for Black Lives*, August 1, 2016, policy .m4bl.org.

21. Robin D.G. Kelley, "What Does Black Lives Matter Want?," *Boston Review*, August 17, 2016, bostonreview.net.

22. Movement for Black Lives, "Economic Justice," August 1, 2016, policy .m4bl.org.

23. Patrice Marie Cullors-Brignac, "We Didn't Start a Movement. We Started a Network," *Medium*, February 22, 2016, medium.com.

24. Beth Hawkins, "The Movement's Been Hijacked: A Black Lives Matter Leader Quits over Public School Reform," *The 74 Million*, September 7, 2016, the74million.org.

25. Cedric Johnson, "Afterword: Baltimore, the Policing Crisis and the End of the Obama Era," in James DeFilippis, ed., *Urban Policy in the Time of Obama* (Minneapolis: University of Minnesota Press, 2016), 302–21.

26. Michelle Alexander, *The New Jim Crow: Mass Incarceration in the Age of Colorblindness* (New York: New Press, 2010).

27. For critical treatments of Alexander's work, see Marie Gottschalk, *Caught: The Prison State and the Lockdown of American Politics* (Princeton,

NJ: Princeton University Press, 2015), 3–7, 119–67; and James Forman Jr., "Racial Critiques of Mass Incarceration: Beyond the New Jim Crow," *New York University Law Review* 87 (February 2012), 101–46.

28. Loïc Wacquant, "Class, Race and Hyperincarceration in Revanchist America," *Daedalus* 139, no. 3 (Summer 2010): 78; Loïc Wacquant, *Punishing the Poor: The Neoliberal Government of Social Insecurity* (Durham, NC: Duke University Press, 2009).

29. "The Counted: People Killed by Police in the U.S.," *Guardian*, interactive database, theguardian.com; see also Lester Spence, "Policing Class," *Jacobin*, August 16, 2016, jacobinmag.com; Adolph Reed Jr., "How Racial Disparity Does Not Help Make Sense of Patterns of Police Violence," *Nonsite*, September 16, 2016, nonsite.org.

30. "The Struggle for Racial Justice Has a Long Way to Go: Michelle Alexander interviewed by Matt Pillischer," *International Socialist Review* 84 (June 2012).

2 Black Political Life and the Blue Lives Matter Presidency

1. Mychal Denzel Smith, "The Rebirth of Black Rage," *The Nation*, August 13, 2015, thenation.com.

2. Thomas J. Adams, "How the Ruling Class Remade New Orleans," *Jacobin*, August 2015.

3. Asad Haider, *Mistaken Identity* (London and New York: Verso, 2018).

4. Combahee River Collective, "The Combahee River Collective Statement" (1977), in *How We Get Free: Black Feminism and the Combahee River Collective*, ed. Keeanga-Yamahtta Taylor (Chicago: Haymarket, 2017).

5. Haider, *Mistaken Identity*, 12.

6. Ibid.

7. Asad Haider, "Zombie Manifesto," Verso blog, September 1, 2018, versobooks.com.

8. Haider, *Mistaken Identity*, 11.

9. Ibid., 51.

10. Bran Dougherty-Johnson, "Populist Persuasions," *Baffler*, October 31, 2018, thebaffler.com.

11. Neil Smith, *The New Urban Frontier: Gentrification and the Revanchist City* (London: Routledge, 1996).

12. Ibid., 44–5.

13. Mike Davis, *City of Quartz: Excavating the Future in Los Angeles* (London and New York: Verso, 1990), 226.
14. James Forman Jr., *Locking Up Our Own* (New York: Farrar, Straus and Giroux, 2017).

3 Only a Class Politics Can Save Us from Police Violence and Fascism: Lessons from Rosa Luxemburg and Cedric Johnson

1. Rosa Luxemburg, "The Polish Question at the International Congress in London" (1896), in Horace B. Davis, ed., *The National Question: Selected Writings by Rosa Luxemburg* (New York: Monthly Review, 1976); Rosa Luxemburg, "The Russian Revolution," in Mary-Alice Waters, ed., *Rosa Luxemburg Speaks* (New York: Pathfinder Press, 1970). See also her article on the ineffectiveness of Polish nationalists in combating the oppression of Poles in eastern Germany and the necessity of united, cross-ethnic, working-class solidarity as the only effective weapon: Rosa Luxemburg, "In Defense of Nationality" (1900), translated by Emal Ghamsharick for Marxists' Internet Archive, esp. Section 4, "Nobility, Bourgeoisie and People in Poznan Province," marxists.org.
2. Luxemburg, "The Russian Revolution," 502–3.
3. Cedric Johnson, "The Panthers Can't Save Us Now," *Catalyst* 1, no. 1 (Spring 2017), Chapter 1 in this volume.
4. Cited in ibid.
5. Ibid.
6. For critical analyses of the Black-led Movement Fund, of which the Garza-Cullors-Tometi Black Lives Matter group is a leading recipient, see "Billionaires Back Black Lives Matter," World Socialist Website, October 11, 2016, wsws.org; Bruce Dixon, "Who Owns the Movement and Where Are They Taking It?," *Black Agenda Report*, January 12, 2017, blackagendareport.com; Paul Street, "What Would the Black Panthers Think of Black Lives Matter?," *Truthdig*, October 29, 2017, truthdig.com. For the list of fund recipients, see "Black-led Movement Fund," Borealis Philanthropy, borealisphilanthropy.org. On the groups that came together for the vision statement, see "About Us," Movement for Black Lives, m4bl.org.
7. On growing intra-racial inequality among African Americans, see the study published by Credit Suisse and Brandeis University's Institute on

Assets and Social Policy (IASP), "Wealth Patterns among the Top 5 percent of African-Americans," November 2014.

8. Rosa Luxemburg, "The Mass Strike, the Political Party, and the Trade Unions," in Waters, *Rosa Luxemburg Speaks*, 285.

9. Johnson, "Panthers Can't Save Us Now."

10. Bayard Rustin, " 'Black Power' and Coalition Politics," *Commentary*, September 1966, 36.

11. Rosa Luxemburg, "The Junius Pamphlet: The Crisis in the German Social Democratic Party," in Waters, *Rosa Luxemburg Speaks*, 357.

12. Ibid., 348, emphasis added.

4 In Defense of Black Sentiment: A Comment on Cedric Johnson's Essay Re: Black Power Nostalgia

1. C.L.R. James, *A History of Pan-African Revolt*, 2nd rev. ed. (Washington, DC: Spear Press, 1969).

2. See Alexander Weheliye, *Habeas Viscus: Racializing Assemblages, Biopolitics, and Black Feminist Theories of the Human* (Durham, NC: Duke University Press, 2014).

3. Ibid.

4. Ibid.

5. Ruth Wilson Gilmore, *Golden Gulag: Prisons, Surplus, Crisis, and Opposition in Globalizing California* (Berkeley: University of California Press, 2007).

6. See Katherine McKittrick, *Sylvia Wynter on Being Human as Praxis* (Durham, NC: Duke University Press, 2014).

7. Lisa Lowe, *The Intimacies of Four Continents* (Durham, NC: Duke University Press, 2015).

8. George Ciccariello-Maher, *Decolonizing Dialectics* (Durham, NC: Duke University Press, 2017).

9. Adolph Reed, "Race and the Disruption of the New Deal Coalition," *Urban Affairs Quarterly* 27, no. 2 (1991): 326–33; Eric Rauchway, *The Great Depression and the New Deal: A Very Short Introduction* (New York: Oxford University Press, 2008).

10. Ciccariello-Maher, *Decolonizing Dialectics*, 11.

11. For an example of the dominant scholarship, see Brady Thomas Heiner, "Foucault and the Black Panthers," *City* 11, no. 3 (2007): 313–56.

12. Nik Heynen, "Bending the Bars of Empire from Every Ghetto for Survival: The Black Panther Party's Radical Anti-hunger Politics of Social Reproduction and Scale," *Annals of the Association of American Geographers* 99, no. 2 (2009): 406–22.

13. Alondra Nelson, *Body and Soul: The Black Panther Party and the Fight against Medical Discrimination* (Minneapolis: University of Minnesota Press, 2013).

14. Alana Lentin, "Thinking Blackly: Beyond Biopolitics and Bare Life," March 22, 2017, *Alana Lentin* (blog), alanalentin.net.

15. W.E.B. Du Bois, cited in Tommie Shelby, *We Who Are Dark* (Cambridge, MA: Harvard University Press, 2009).

16. Ibid.

17. See Gilmore, *Golden Gulag*.

5 Black Exceptionalism and the Militant Capitulation to Economic Inequality

1. Josiah Rector, "Neoliberalism's Deadly Experiment," *Jacobin*, October 16, 2016, jacobinmag.com.

2. Fareed Zakaria, "America's Self-Destructive Whites," *Washington Post*, December 31, 2015, washingtonpost.com.

3. Ibid.

4. Ibid.

5. Cherrie Bucknor, "Black Workers, Unions, and Inequality," Center for Economic Policy and Research, cepr.net.

6. Bayard Rustin, " 'Black Power' and Coalition Politics," *Commentary*, September 1966.

6 Cedric Johnson and the Other Sixties' Nostalgia

1. Cedric Johnson, "The Panthers Can't Save Us Now," *Catalyst* 1, no. 1 (Spring 2017); Cedric Johnson, "Black Political Life and the Blue Lives Matter Presidency," *New Politics* 66 (Winter 2019); see Chapters 1 and 2 in this volume.

2. Johnson, "Panthers Can't Save Us Now," 84.

3. Touré F. Reed, "Black Exceptionalism and the Militant Capitulation to Economic Inequality," *New Politics* 66 (Winter 2019).

4. See, for instance, Manning Marable, *Black American Politics* (London: Verso, 1985).

5. All figures for jail and prison are from 2018 US Department of Justice reports. In these reports, an important distinction is made between those considered "white" and "non-Hispanic whites," which gives a clearer picture of the role of race.

6. Johnson, "Panthers Can't Save Us Now," 83.

7. Quoted in Herbert Garfinkel, *When Negroes March* (New York: Anetheum, 1969).

8. Bayard Rustin, "From Protest to Politics: The Future of the Civil Rights Movement," *Commentary*, February 1965.

9. Johnson, "Panthers Can't Save Us Now," 66.

10. One of the best answers to Rustin's "From Protest to Politics" at that time appeared in *New Politics* 5, no. 4 (Fall 1966), 47–65, by its editor Julius Jacobson under the mocking title of "From Protest to Politicking."

11. The essays originally appeared in *New Politics* 66 (Winter 2019); Mia White's is reproduced as Chapter 4 in this volume.

7 *What Black Life Actually Looks Like*

1. See Cedric Johnson, "Black Political Life and the Blue Lives Matter Presidency," *New Politics* 66 (Winter 2019), Chapter 2 in this volume.

2. Mia White, "In Defense of Black Sentiment A Comment on Cedric Johnson's Essay Re: Black Power Nostalgia," *New Politics* 66 (Winter 2019), Chapter 4 in this volume.

3. Kim Moody, "Cedric Johnson and the Other Sixties' Nostalgia," *New Politics*, March 1, 2019, newpolitics.org, Chapter 6 in this volume.

4. See James Forman Jr., *Locking Up Our Own* (New York: Farrar, Straus and Giroux, 2017); Michael Javen Fortner, *Black Silent Majority: The Rockefeller Drug Laws and the Politics of Punishment* (Cambridge, MA: Harvard University Press, 2015); Donna Murch, "Crack in Los Angeles: Crisis, Militarization, and Black Response to the Late Twentieth-Century War on Drugs," *Journal of American History* 102, no. 1 (June 2015): 162–73.

5. Stuart Hall et al., *Policing the Crisis: Mugging, the State and Law and Order* (London: Palgrave-Macmillan, 2013 [1978]); Ruth Wilson Gilmore, *Golden Gulag: Prisons, Surplus, Crisis, and Opposition in Globalizing*

California (Berkeley: University of California Press, 2007); Theodore G. Chiricos and Miriam A. Delone, "Labor Surplus and Punishment: A Review and Assessment of Theory and Evidence," *Social Problems* 39, no. 4 (November 1992): 421–46; Todd Gordon, "The Political-Economy of Law-and-Order Policies: Policing, Class Struggle, and Neoliberal Restructuring," *Studies in Political Economy* 75 (Spring 2005), 53–77.

6. Loïc Waquant, "Class, Race and Hyperincarceration in Revanchist America," *Socialism and Democracy* 28 (2014).

7. Brett Story, "The Prison in the City: Tracking the Neoliberal Life of the 'Million Dollar Block,' " *Theoretical Criminology* 20, no. 3 (2016): 257–76.

8. Employing the *National Longitudinal Study of Adolescents to Adult Health*, Nathaniel Lewis has found that "class appears to be a larger factor than usually reported when studying racial disparities" and surprisingly for some, "race is not statistically significant factor for many incarceration outcomes, once class is adequately controlled for." See Nathaniel Lewis, "Mass Incarceration: New Jim Crow, Class War or Both?," *People's Policy Project*, January 30, 2018, peoplespolicyproject .org; Nathaniel Lewis, "Locking Up the Lower Class," *Jacobin*, January 30, 2018, jacobinmag.com.

9. Karl Marx, *Capital: A Critique of Political Economy*, vol. 1 (London: Penguin, 1990).

10. Lucius Couloute and Daniel Kopf, "Out of Prison and Out of Work: Unemployment among formerly Incarcerated People," Prison Policy Initiative, July 2018, prisonpolicy.org; Bernadette Rabuy and Daniel Kopf, "Prisons of Poverty: Uncovering the Pre-incarceration Incomes of the Imprisoned," Prison Policy Initiative, July 9, 2015, prisonpolicy .org; Adam Looney and Nicholas Turner, "Work and Opportunity before and after Incarceration," Brookings Institution, March 2018, brookings.edu.

11. Zhandarka Kurti describes this process in some detail, while remarking on the futility of probation as a reformist strategy given the fact of structural unemployment: "The requirements to find work and housing and to avoid contact with the police are often basic conditions. The few people who meet these conditions are mostly funneled to low-wage work in the service industry. Probation officers are ill equipped to find people jobs; they can only recommend numerous job-training and workforce programs in the hopes that participating in these dissuade

young folks from a life of crime . . . Today more than ever, the idea that work can transform 'criminals' into 'productive citizens' is dubious at best. Increased economic insecurity and low-wage jobs make 'productive citizenship,' the penal-welfarist goal on which probation was founded, seem like a pipe dream. Instead, the function of community supervision resembles more that of the prison: a way to manage poverty and growing surplus populations in deindustrialized urban cores. The success of second chance programs that rely heavily on probation depends not on how well rigid organizational bureaucracies embrace 'change,' which is how many liberal reformers frame it, but the extent to which each state and county can absorb surplus populations." Zhandarka Kurti, "Second Chances in the Era of the Jobless Future," *Brooklyn Rail*, March 5, 2018.

12. Jamie Peck and Nik Theodore, "Carceral Chicago: Making the Ex-offender Employability Crisis," *International Journal of Urban and Regional Research* 32, no. 3 (June 2008): 251–81.

13. Neil Smith, *The New Urban Frontier: Gentrification and the Revanchist City* (London: Routledge, 1996); Neil Smith, "Revanchist Planet: Regeneration and the Axis of Co-Evilism," Urban Reinventors Paper Series, 2005–2009, urbanreinventors.net; Mike Davis, *City of Quartz: Excavating the Future in Los Angeles* (London: Verso, 1990); Don Mitchell, "Against Safety, Against Security: Reinvigorating Urban Life," in Michael J. Thompson, ed., *Fleeing the City: Studies in the Culture and Politics of Antiurbanism* (New York: Palgrave-Macmillan, 2009), 233–48; Timothy Gibson, *Securing the Spectacular City: The Politics of Revitalization and Homelessness in Downtown Seattle* (Lanham, MD: Lexington Books, 2004); Alex Vitale, *City of Disorder: How the Quality of Life Campaign Transformed New York Politics* (New York: New York University Press, 2008); Ayobami Laniyonu, "Coffee Shops and Street Stops: Policing Practices in Gentrifying Neighborhoods," *Urban Affairs Review* 54, no. 5 (2018): 898–930; Elaine B. Sharp, "Politics, Economics and Urban Policing: The Postindustrial City Thesis and Rival Explanations of Heightened Order Maintenance Policing," *Urban Affairs Review* 50, no. 3 (2013): 340–65; Stuart Forrest, *Down, Out and Under Arrest: Policing and Everyday Life in Skid Row* (Chicago: University of Chicago, 2016).

14. Eli Hager, "A Mass Incarceration Mystery," *Marshall Project*, December 15, 2017, themarshallproject.org.

15. Ira Katznelson, *When Affirmative Action Was White: An Untold Story of Twentieth Century Racial Inequality in Twentieth Century America* (New York and London: W.W. Norton, 2005); Ta-Nehisi Coates, "The Case for Reparations," *Atlantic*, June 2014.

16. Touré F. Reed, "Between Obama and Coates," *Catalyst* 1, no. 4 (Winter 2018).

17. See Neil M. Maher, *Nature's New Deal: The Civilian Conservation Corps and the Roots of the American Environmental Movement* (New York: Oxford University Press, 2008); Nick Taylor, *American-Made: The Enduring Legacy of the WPA: When FDR Put the Nation to Work* (New York: Bantam, 2009).

18. Nick Taylor, *American-Made*, TK.

19. Luther C. Wandall, "A Negro in the CCC," *Crisis* 42 (August 1935): 244, 253–54.

20. Another favored target of the "constraint of race" discourse is the GI Bill. I can't say how many times in the last decade I've had a student in my courses, or an audience participant after a lecture, make the claim that blacks did not benefit from the GI Bill's provisions. This claim runs a close second to the myth about Social Security as a rhetorical move to short-circuit any talk of fighting for universal public policy in our times. Suzanne Mettler offers a healing balm against this contagion. In her study of the GI Bill and African American veterans, she concludes: "Contrary to the assumption that African Americans had little access to the G. I. Bill, Veterans' Administration records verify that, over the first five years of the program, higher proportions of nonwhites than whites used the law's education and training benefits . . . [By] 1950 49 percent of nonwhite veterans had used the benefit compared to 43 percent of white veterans. The provisions were used at especially high rates in the South, where 51 percent of all veterans had entered some kind of education or training by 1950. Strikingly, nonwhite southern veteran's usage surpassed that of white veterans in the region, at 56 percent compared to 50 percent. Similarly, in the West, 46 percent of nonwhite veterans went to school on the G. I. Bill, compared to 42 percent of white veterans. Nationwide, black World War II veterans numbered 1,308,000; already by 1950, 640,920 of them had benefited from the G.I. Bill's education and training provisions." Suzanne Mettler, " 'The Only Good Thing Was the G. I. Bill': Effects of the Education and Training Provisions on African-American Veterans' Political Participation," *Studies in American*

Political Development 19 (Spring 2005): 31–52. See also Michael J. Bennett, *When Dreams Came True: The GI Bill and the Making of Modern America* (Washington, DC: Brassey's, 1996).

21. Lizabeth Cohen, *Making a New Deal: Industrial Workers in Chicago, 1919–1939* (Cambridge, UK: Cambridge University Press, 1990); Ahmed White, *The Last Great Strike: Little Steel, the CIO and the Struggle for Labor Rights in New Deal America* (Oakland: University of California, 2016); Charles D. Chamberlain, *Victory at Home: Manpower and Race in the American South during World War II* (Athens and London: University of Georgia Press, 2003).

22. See William P. Jones, *The March on Washington: Jobs, Freedom, and the Forgotten History of Civil Rights* (New York: W.W. Norton, 2013).

23. See Rhonda F. Levine, *Class Struggle and the New Deal: Industrial Labor, Industrial Capital and the State* (Lawrence: University of Kansas, 1988); Meg Jacobs, " 'Democracy's Third Estate': New Deal Politics and the Construction of a 'Consuming Public,' " *International Labor and Working-Class History* 55 (Spring 1999): 27–51.

24. See Judith Stein, *Running Steel, Running America: Race, Economic Policy, and the Decline of Liberalism* (Chapel Hill: University of North Carolina Press, 1998).

25. Stephen Steinberg, "Bayard Rustin and the Rise and Decline of the Black Protest Movement," *New Politics* 23 (Summer 1997).

26. Bayard Rustin, "From Protest to Politics: The Future of the Civil Rights Movement," *Commentary*, February 1965.

27. Gregor Baszak, "Marxism through the Back Door: An Interview with Cedric Johnson," *Platypus* 79 (September 2015).

28. See Christian Weller, "Only Large Policy Interventions Such as Reparations Can Shrink the Racial Wealth Gap," *Forbes*, March 21, 2019, forbes.com; David Brooks, "The Case for Reparations," *New York Times*, March 7, 2019.